10·25·77

FRED E. CASE is Professor of Real Estate
and Urban Land Economics,
Graduate School of Management,
University of California,
Los Angeles.

THE INVESTMENT GUIDE TO HOME & LAND PURCHASE

|||||||||||||||||||||||||||||||||||||||||||||||||||||||||||||||||||||||||||||||||||||||||||||||||||||||||||||||||||||||||||||||||||||||

FRED E. CASE

A SPECTRUM BOOK

PRENTICE-HALL, INC., Englewood Cliffs, New Jersey 07632

Library of Congress Cataloging in Publication Data
Case, Frederick E
    The investment guide to home and land purchase.

    (A Spectrum Book)
    Includes index.
    1. House buying.   I. Title.
HD1379.C317   643   77-24751
ISBN 0-13-502674-1
ISBN 0-13-502666-0 pbk.

© 1977 by Prentice-Hall, Inc., Englewood Cliffs, New Jersey 07632

A Spectrum Book

10 9 8 7 6 5 4 3 2 1

Printed in the United States of America

PRENTICE-HALL INTERNATIONAL, INC., *London*
PRENTICE-HALL OF AUSTRALIA PTY. LIMITED, *Sydney*
PRENTICE-HALL OF CANADA, LTD., *Toronto*
PRENTICE-HALL OF INDIA PRIVATE LIMITED, *New Delhi*
PRENTICE-HALL OF JAPAN, INC., *Tokyo*
PRENTICE-HALL OF SOUTHEAST ASIA PTE. LTD., *Singapore*
WHITEHALL BOOKS LIMITED, *Wellington, New Zealand*

CONTENTS

||||||||||||||||||||||||||||||||||||||||||||||||||||||||||||||||||||||||||||||||||||||||||||||||||||||||||||||||||||||||||||||||

1998389

PREFACE

Buying a home is an unaffordable luxury for some and an impossible financial strain for too many familes. On the other hand, if a family can acquire a home, it becomes a solid foundation for creating a financial reserve that will be available in emergencies and that will be a useful base for future retirement planning.

The materials in this book have been developed over the last ten years because so many people have asked me, "Should I buy a home?" "Should I buy one now?" Answers to these and so many other similar questions were presented at many seminars and informal gatherings. The information was used to present twenty half-hour shows for N.B.C. Parts of the materials have been published in newspapers from Maine to California.

The book is planned to provide guidance to you in evaluating homes that you might want to purchase, with the emphasis on the kinds of yestions you should ask and to which you should receive "yes" answers. You can turn to any section of the book and use it without reading the other parts. In the process, you can develop number scores that will help you to compare homes or to decide whether a particular home is a good investment for your family.

Look at the process of selecting and buying a home as a "fun game" with a valuable financial prize as a permanent reward. I assume that everyone should "get a lot" and that your home need not be a "hassle." This is a game you can play like an expert if you keep this book beside you to help you develop your strategies for making every home you buy a rewarding investment experience.

GETTING READY TO USE HOME OWNERSHIP TO BUILD YOUR FAMILY ESTATE

‖‖‖

1

Over one half of all families in the United States own homes and most of those families have or are now making money through that ownership. Most realize a profit more by accident than by intent. Even those who plan to make a profit do not realize all that they might from this form of investment.

Unfortunately, more and more families are being discouraged from home ownership because they feel that they cannot afford to buy, let alone maintain their homes. On the other hand, knowledgeable investors are constantly buying all kinds of real estate because of the high earning potentials.

In this book I suggest how you can use a combination of your good common sense and some expert help to buy the home your family wants and needs and make good profits just as the experts do.

The formula for using home ownership to build a family financial estate is relatively easy to follow but does require following a proper sequence of events. You must also be willing to do a modest amount of hard work yourself and learn how to use and pay for the expert services of appraisers, lawyers, lenders, and others.

In very brief outline, these are the factors we believe you should understand in the order in which you should use them to make your home your fortune. (Figure 1-1):

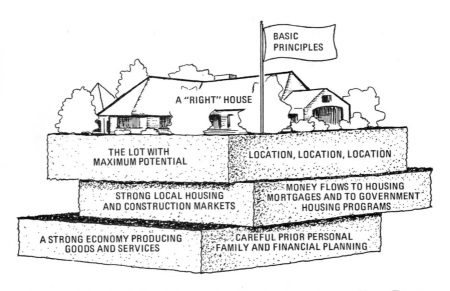

Figure 1-1   Building Blocks For Making Your Home Your Fortune

1. Do some careful family financial planning (Chapters 1–4).
2. Time your investment to take advantage of changes in the economy and the costs of borrowed money (Chapter 5).
3. Study your local housing markets and use market changes to your advantage (Chapter 6).
4. Find the "best" location and the best home in that location (Chapter 7).

5. Inspect the lot and the house carefully, looking for its investment value increase potentials (Chapter 8).
6. Use experts to help you plan and execute your home investment program (Chapters 9, 10, 11).
7. When you are financially ready, prepare to move into other kinds of real estate investments (Chapters 12, 13).
8. Keep reviewing the basic principles and follow them in all of your real estate investments (Chapter 14).

WHY A HOME CAN BE A GOOD INVESTMENT

When you borrow to buy your home, the lenders will be charging you between 8 and 10 per cent interest per year on your loan because they consider home loans to be good, safe investments. If they find that homes are good investments and can earn such rates, why shouldn't you plan to earn as much as they do? Actually, with careful planning and management, you should be able to earn as much as 20 to 40 per cent annually on the money you invest in your home.

To help you understand why this is possible I present an example of how the proper planning and managing of your home can produce high rates of return on your equity without undue risk. Do not be worried about calculations which you see in Table 1-1; if you can do basic arithmetic, you can do them easily. Follow the discussion which relates to this table; then, in Table 1-2, use the same instructions to calculate what the investment value of your home might be.

Before we begin, however, we wish to emphasize the conditions which we have assumed would exist in order for this home to be such a good investment:

1. The home fits your family living style.
2. The home is in an area where values are increasing at least 5 per cent each year.
3. You used real estate brokers and appraisers to establish a price for the house which is the proper "market" price.
4. You borrowed the maximum which the lender would allow, in this case 80 per cent of the purchase price.

Table 1-1 Investment Buildup Potential in a Single-Family Home (5-year holding period)

	Initial Purchase (in dollars)	End of Year (in dollars) 1	2	3	4	5	TOTALS
A. Current market price	40,000	42,000	44,100	46,305	48,620	51,051	
B. Transfer costs	400						
C. Total investment price	40,400						
D. Down payment, costs paid	8,400						
D. Amount to be mortgaged	32,000						
Costs of Owning, Using							
E. Mortgage payment	257.48	3,098	3,098	3,098	3,098	3,098	15,943
Principal		218	239	261	286	312	1,813
Interest		2,871	2,850	2,828	2,803	2,776	14,130
F. Property Taxes		1,155	1,212	1,273	1,337	1,403	6,382
G. Property Insurance		420	441	463	486	510	2,320
H. Maintenance		525	551	578	607	638	2,899
I. Utilities, using costs		105	110	115	121	127	578
J. Total cash outlay		5,303	5,412	5,527	5,770	5,776	28,122
Investment Position							
K. EQUITY BUILDUP							
Market price increase		2,000	2,100	2,205	2,315	2,431	11,051
Mortgage principal		218	239	261	286	312	1,316
(EQUITY BUILDUP)		2,218	2,339	2,466	2,601	2,743	12,367
L. TAX SHELTERED INCOME (40% income tax bracket)							
Federal income tax							
Mortgage interest		1,148	1,140	1,131	1,121	1,110	6,798
Property taxes		462	484	509	534	561	2,650
(TAX SHELTERED INCOME)		1,610	1,624	1,640	1,655	1,671	9,448
M. Total Equity Buildup		3,828	3,963	4,106	4,256	4,416	20,569
Minus: Loss of interest on $8,000 equity (5.75% earnings on savings loss)		−460	−486	−514	−544	−575	−2,579
Total Improved Investment Position		3,368	3,477	3,592	3,712	3,841	17,990
$\dfrac{\text{Improved investment position}}{\text{accumulated equity}}$ = Return on equity		42%	31%	24%	20%	17%	81%
(accumulated equity)		8,000	11,368	14,845	18,437	22,278	22,278
Accumulated Total Equity							22,278

5. You used an income-tax advisor to help you get all of the "tax-sheltered income" legally available to you.
6. You plan to move to a better investment home by "trading up" rather than selling and buying.

Perhaps these conditions may sound strange to you or even impossible for you to follow. Please read on. They are some basic ideas which you will grasp easily. Your problem will be in learning how to use them properly.

In Table 1-1 we have assumed that you are earning about $20,000 per year and that you have purchased a $40,000 home, paying $8,000 down and borrowing $32,000. The loan has an annual 9 per cent interest rate and a 30-year term which means you will be paying $257.48 per month on the loan. (In Chapter 3 I show you how to calculate your loan payment, in Chapter 4 how to shop for the best loan terms.)

To estimate what your home will cost to own and operate you should relate the costs to the current market value of your home. In this example we are using percentages that are average for most of the country; however, you will want to check these against the experiences of home owners in your area and adjust them to fit your market areas. In calculating the costs, we use the expected value increase at the end of the year to estimate costs for the year. This helps you anticipate the impact of inflation. For example, we have assumed that you purchased the home for $40,000 and that the value increased by 5 per cent during the year, so that at the end of the first year the value would be $42,000. We used $42,000 to calculate the costs of ownership during your first year of occupancy.

Although you have paid $8,000 as a down payment, you must also pay cash closing costs of $400. (In Chapter 2 I indicate how you can keep these costs as low as possible.)

Your costs of owning and using the home and your earning potentials during a five-year period are estimated on an annual basis as follows (Table 1-1, items E through J):

1. Monthly mortgage payments on principal and
interest for the year $3,098

2.	Property taxes (assumed to equal 3 per cent of the current market value)	1,155
3.	Property insurance: full coverage, owner's liability and fire (1 per cent of market value)	420
4.	Maintaining the property and the equipment: heating, plumbing, and so on (1.25 per cent of market value)	525
5.	Utilities and other occupancy and using costs (0.25 per cent of market value)	105
Total annual cash outlay		$5,303

An annual cash outlay of $5,303 is more than 25 per cent of your annual income of $20,000, which may seem more than you can afford. Wait—there is good news coming.

At this point your investment in the property equals the $2,000 down payment and the $218 you have paid on the loan principal. We assumed that you would be in the 40 per cent income tax bracket; however, whatever your bracket may be, you can deduct from the income which you would normally report for tax purposes the cash you paid on the mortgage interest and the property taxes, which are $2,871 and $1,155, for a total of $4,026. You can deduct the entire $4,026 from your income before you estimate your income-tax liability. If you did not have this amount to deduct, you would have reported $4,026 in earnings and would have paid a tax equal to 40 per cent of this, or $1,610. Instead, you save the payment of $1,610 which means you now have that much tax-sheltered income. Instead of a cash outlay of $5,303 for home ownership, you now have only ($5,303 minus $1,610) $3,693, which means that your home has cost you only 18 per cent of your income. Most families pay about 20 per cent. Added to the equity you already have of $2,218, your total equity buildup is now $3,828.

However, in paying $8,000 down on the home, you have denied yourself the opportunity of earning interest on that amount by depositing it in a savings and loan account. If your local savings and loan associations were paying 5.75 per cent annually on savings, you would lose $460, so we subtract that from your current total equity of $3,828 to get $3,368.

At the end of the year your equity buildup of $3,368 represents a

42-per-cent return on your original down payment of $8,000. Of course, you can't spend this, nor can you be sure you have really earned it until you sell the home and pay the costs of the sale.

If, during the 5 years of ownership, your home costs continued about the way we calculated them for the first year, at the end of the fifth year you would have improved your equity position by $17,990 and your total equity would be $22,278, compared to the original $8,000 you paid. In other words, your total return on your accumulated equity at the end of the fifth year would be 81 per cent, or an annual average of 16.2 per cent (81 per cent divided by 5 years).

Can you do this easily? Real estate does fluctuate in value, and the costs of owning homes are rising. All that we can say at this point is that this is what was happening to the "average" home owner in the years between 1970 and 1975. We have no way of guaranteeing that this will continue to be true. I do say that by following the ideas offered in the remaining portions of this book, you will have an excellent chance of earning the maximum amount possible on your own.

Remember also that these earnings are paper earnings. The difficult task is to translate your paper plans to a real home investment. This is the very basic purpose of this book. This is also why real-estate investment planning and management is different from that for other kinds of investments. There are some special things about real-estate investments that you must understand. On the other hand, once you have mastered these ideas, you can take personal charge of seeing that your investments behave according to your plans, something you cannot do with stocks or bonds.

Perhaps you would want to try estimating your costs of home ownership. Table 1-2 is provided for this purpose, with some suggestions of how to estimate your costs and potentials.

RENTING AS A PRELUDE TO BUYING

Perhaps you do not now nor ever have owned a home but are wondering whether you could use home ownership for investment purposes. There are problems in owning a home which you may not wish to face even though you could make money through ownership. In Table 1-3 is a brief checklist you can use to decide whether home ownership would be too much for you at present. If you use the checklist and find that you end up with more "nos" than "yesses," don't give up the idea of ownership but decide to do some productive waiting until you have overcome some of the problems represented by your "no" list.

Table 1-2A Estimating the Investment Buildup Potentials in a Single-Family Home

A. *Current market price:* Visit some of the local real estate offices and ask them what they would sell the home for. Average their estimates and then deduct about 5 per cent on the assumption that they will be optimistic in order to have the opportunity to list your home for sale. In some areas your local property tax bill will indicate what the assessor thinks your home would sell for. Normally, this is 5 or 10 per cent below the actual sales price. Be sure to check the date on which the assessed value was established. To estimate annual price changes discuss with the local real estate agents what has been happening to the prices of properties they have been selling. Use their past experiences as a basis for estimating what the future annual changes will be.

B. *Transfer costs:* When you sell your home you will have to pay a sales commission of 5 to 7 per cent, depending upon local custom. You caι negotiate this percentage with the selling agents, but check first to see what others have been paying. There will be incidental costs of transferring title and completing other kinds of legal arrangements. Again, real estate sales agents can give you estimates of this. You can also check with the home-loan officer in your local bank or savings association, title insurance companies, escrow companies, abstract, and title companies.

C. *Down payment and loan costs:* Check with several home loan officers in your
D. local lending institutions. Loan terms—down payment, length of loan, in-
E. terest rate, and loan costs—do vary among lenders, so shop around. Use an average.

F. *Property taxes:* Ask to see the tax bills over the last five years if possible, and take an average, knowing that taxes will probably go up.

G. *Property insurance:* There are many kinds of insurance programs for home owners. Check with more than one local insurance agent to determine what you should include in your program and what the annual costs will be.

H. *Maintenance:* What you spend for operating and maintaining is largely your choice. Whenever you have major work to be done, try to get at least three

Table 1-2A *(cont.)*

estimates. The quality of materials in the home and your local climatic conditions will determine what you have to do. When you are looking at a home, ask the current owners to show their bills to give you a list of the major repairs, improvements, and replacements they have completed. This will give you an idea of whether the home has been maintained and what additional work you may face. In many cities you can call city hall and ask for a building code inspection. This will tell of any repairs which will have to be done. More and more real estate agents provide home-warranty insurance. For a single payment you receive a guarantee as to the quality of major items in the home and the assurance that any repairs to them will be paid for by the insurer if defects are uncovered during the life of the policy.

I. *Utilities and other using costs:* Ask the current owners to provide you copies of their utility and other service bills for the last year at least, preferably for several years. If they will not or cannot furnish them, check with local utility companies for estimates on water, electricity, gas, sewer charges, and trash collection charges; check city hall for any special user charges or special assessment charges for the area in which you are buying.

L. *Tax-sheltered income:* Visit an income tax specialist who understands what kinds of records you should keep and what kinds of tax deductions you can take. You can also obtain from your local Internal Revenue Service office the latest taxpayers' guide which will tell you what your rights are as a home owner. An important item is to keep records of all expenses in buying and using your home during your entire period of ownership.

Table 1-2B Investment Buildup Potential
In a Single-Family Home

Initial Purchase

A.	Current market price	_____
B.	Transfer costs	_____
	Total investment price	_____
C.	Down payment, cost paid	_____
D.	Amount to be mortgaged	_____

Costs of Owning, Using

E.	Mortgage payment	
	Principal	_____
	Interest	_____
F.	Property taxes	_____
G.	Property insurance	_____

Table 1-2B *(cont.)*

H.	Maintenance	_____
I.	Utilities, using costs	_____
J.	Total cash outlay	_____

Investment Position

K.	Equity Buildup	_____
	Market price increase	_____
	Mortgage principal	_____
L.	Tax-sheltered income	_____
	(40% income tax bracket)	
	Federal income tax	_____
	Mortgage interest	_____
	Property taxes	_____
M.	Total equity buildup	
	Minus: Loss of interest on	
	$8,000 equity (5.75% earnings	
	on savings loss)	_____

Total Improved Investment Position

$$\frac{\text{Improved investment position}}{\text{accumulated equity}} = \begin{array}{l}\text{Return} \\ \text{on equity}\end{array} \qquad \text{_____}$$

Accumulated Total Equity   _____

Table 1-3   Should I Buy or Rent?

Score Card: Good—10 yeses;   Acceptable—9 yeses;   Poor—8 or less

You may have a very firm opinion about the wisdom of buying a house, in which case you can skip this section. However, home ownership is not for everyone and you should be sure to consider the problems as well as the joys of home ownership. Score yourself on the following chart and then compare your score with the score card above. If you score low, you may want to reconsider developing a real estate investment program through home buying. In this case, go to the section on analyzing income properties.

Table 1-3 *(cont.)*

		YES	NO
1.	Is my job permanent enough to let me live in one place at least 2 years?	✓	
2.	Do I know how much space my family needs as a result of previous rental or home ownership experience?	✓	
3.	Does my family want to live in a house?	✓	
4.	Do we know who will take care of the lawn, shrubbery, garden, and so on?	✓	
5.	Are we prepared to pay for repairs, redecoration, and alterations around the house?	✓	
6.	Are we willing to be concerned with water bills, tax bills, and property insurance bills?	✓	
7.	Can we buy the house without using all of our cash resources?		✓
8.	Are we prepared to compromise some of our ideas about a home in order to acquire a home within our financial limitations?	✓	
9.	Are we willing to remain among the same neighbors in the same area for a number of years?	✓	
10.	Are we willing to spend more per month for all of the costs of home ownership than our current monthly rental payments?		✓
11.	Are we prepared to continue to pay the same size mortgage payments over periods of 15 to 30 years?	✓	
12.	Are we ready to act as our own janitors, maintenance men, and gardeners?	✓	
	TOTAL		

Remember these points if you decide to buy a home:
1. Your mortgage payments can be less than your current rental payments.
2. You will own a piece of property instead of rental receipts.
3. You can later paint, repair, and redecorate your own home whenever you wish.
4. You will have room for children, pets, a family on your own terms.
5. You have freedom to entertain friends and you can control your privacy.
6. You will not have to move because of a change of landlords.
7. Your rent can't be raised.
8. Renting will probably cost you 15 to 25 per cent of your monthly income and the total costs of home ownership will run you between 25 and 35 per cent.

Obviously, I believe that home ownership is a good undertaking for most families so I have summarized some of the reasons why in the listing of points to remember at the end of the checklist. Perhaps you should compare your ''no'' list with these points; you may want to change your mind and plan to buy now. However, if you still say no, I want to discuss some points about using renting as a prelude to buying.

Evaluating the Rental Unit

Begin your search for a rental unit in the general area in which you might want to buy a home. In this way you can use the neighborhood checklist, which I present in Chapter 7, as a means of determining the home value potential of the area. You may even be able to find a home for rent so that you can also test out your interests in dealing with the problems inherent in living in a house. If you want to be doubly careful in checking out the home for rental purposes, use the checklists for measuring the functional or ''livability'' qualities of the home.

In looking for a potential rental, not only can you visit the area, looking for rental signs, but you might also visit some of the local supermarkets and see if they have notices of rental placed on their bulletin boards; or you might put up your own ''rental wanted.'' Many areas have local newspapers, some of which are free, that contain lists of rentals. Stopping in some of the local real estate offices and visiting the mortgage-loan officers of the local banks and savings and loan associations can help. At the extreme you may even want to place an advertisement in the local newspapers, asking for the kind of rental for which you are looking.

If you find rental signs, visit some of the units so that you can develop some feeling about appropriate rental charges. In checking the rents you will want to know:

1. Is some kind of deposit required in addition to the rents?
2. Is there a rental reduction if a term lease is signed?
3. What is included in the rental payment (utilities, use of any available recreational facilities such as a swimming pool, sauna, tennis courts, etc.)?

4. Are there any kinds of assessments that can be added?

5. What kind of notice is given if rents are to be raised and what options do you have if the raises occur?

In addition to the functional items which we suggest that you check (Chapter 5), you may want to check the plumbing, heating, air conditioning and electrical systems. Can you use the appliances that you own, for example?

Storage is always a problem in rental units so you should inventory your needs and compare them with what is offered:

1. Will your car fit conveniently into the parking space provided?

2. Where do your guests park?

3. Is there rough or general storage for trunks and miscellaneous items?

4. In the apartment, is there closet space for clothes, dishes, appliances, books?

Your next job is to match your standards of maintenance and cleanliness against what you see in the apartment building. If the landscaping and interior show signs of neglect, you may find the rents lower but living much more difficult. Visit the back of the unit and find out how trash is handled. Accumulated trash in a messy area should warn you about the standards of maintenance, and the tenants. Inside the apartment, examine the cleanliness of the appliances. If the landlord has not cleaned up after the other tenants and has allowed them to leave a dirty apartment, beware.

One of the biggest problems with rental units is noise and lack of privacy. You should visit an apartment when the other tenants are at home. Then you can check on whether you can hear them talking, moving about, playing radios, tv sets and stereos. Equally important, you can determine how much neighborhood noise there is. Apartments near major traffic arteries, busy commercial or industrial areas, or in airport flight paths can become unbearably noisy as time passes.

One measure of the quality of an apartment is how long the current tenants have lived in the unit. Perhaps you can make discreet inquiries about the tenants or even visit with one or two of them. Brief conversations with them will quickly provide some insights into the good and bad points of living in the apartment.

Finally, there is the lease.[1] Do not sign it until you have read it carefully and make sure you understand every item in it. Most leases are drawn to favor the landlord, so you may find it worthwhile to ask a friendly real estate office or home-loan officer or your local banker to go over it with you. Look for such things as: (1) cash deposits required and how you get them back; (2) what the landlord insurance covers (your insurance agent can help you on this); (3) what the landlord can do about visits to your unit; (4) what you can do about having repairs made, and who pays for them under what conditions; (5) what you can do if you want to "break" the lease; (6) controls over how many can live with you and how many "visitors" you can have and for how long; (7) any costs of other restrictions or requirements for using the extra facilities provided; (8) what improvements you can make, including hanging pictures or placing other items on the walls; (9) pets, and (10) how living restrictions are enforced. Make sure you obtain in writing any changes or special arrangements you make with the landlord because the written agreement prevails over an oral agreement and is usually the only basis on which you can reach a favorable settlement in landlord–tenant disputes.

One of the problems with renting during inflation is that rents are rising so that you may not be able to sign a lease which fixes your rents for a period of time. In that case, be sure to obtain a clear agreement, preferably in writing, stating the conditions under which rents can be raised and what you can do if you do not wish to pay the increase.

COMPROMISES IN HOME BUYING
FOR INVESTMENT PURPOSES

Since our emphasis is on home ownership, we assume that you are ready to start searching for the home which will be the ideal "family" retreat and potential "family investment." After countless

---

[1] If you want to see a lease form that is favorable to the tenant, write to: *Apartment Life Magazine*, Meredith Corporation, 1716 Locust Street, DesMoines, Iowa, 50336. Your local real estate agent will also have copies of approved (legal, that is) leases used by them on behalf of landlords and property owners.

hours of searching, you will find that the "ideal" home you had hoped to find either does not exist or is too expensive for your pocketbook. Do not despair; this always happens, and, in anticipation of this, I have prepared a list of the most frequent compromises you will face (Table 1-4). There may be others, but it is hoped this list presents the most difficult and will help you decide on others not mentioned here.

**Table 1-4   Am I Ready for Real Estate Ownership?
Compromises in Home Buying
for Investment Purposes**

You will discover, after countless hours spent in looking at many homes, that there is probably no single property which fits all of the ideas which you have in your mind. Even if you build your own home you will be disappointed with some aspects of the finished structure. Home buying always requires some compromise on the part of the purchaser. Listed below are some suggestions to guide you in making the more typical compromises with which you must deal:

1. *Location is usually more important than the property* and your best buy will usually be a smaller home in a better location rather than a larger home in a less desirable location.

2. *An older home (15 to 20 years) is preferable to a new home* if you want a lot of space for your money.

3. *Good workmanship with poor materials* is preferable to good materials with poor workmanship and will probably cost you less in repairs and maintenance in the long run.

4. *A low down payment is preferable* if you plan to sell the home in the near future.

5. *A shorter term loan with higher monthly payments* is preferable if you can afford it because this arrangement can reduce the total costs of your new home by one-third to one-half.

6. *A plain house with simple lines* will retain its resale value longer than a house of current but confused architecture.

7. *Currently, a house with at least three or four bedrooms and one and a half to three baths* has the most market appeal and can be sold for the best price.

8. *A house with 1,200 to 1,500 square feet of living area* is usually considered to be a minimum-sized house, even for two people.

9. *Convertibility:* the home should lend itself to changing uses and family lifestyles without requiring substantial remodeling.

Table 1-4 *(cont.)*

10. *An energy-saving potential is more important than style or appearance.* Homes with large amounts of glass area or openness may look better, but consider the extra heat and other utility costs. Put energy-saving potential, including insulation, ahead of external beauty.

11. *A home with the basic repairs and improvements already made* will usually be a better buy than one with a lower price but with many unspecified repairs and improvement needs.

CAN I AFFORD
THIS HOME?

||||||||||||||||||||||||||||||||||||||||||||||||||||||||||||||||||||||||||||||||||||||||||||||||||||||||||||||||||||||||||||||||||||||||||

2

You have no doubt heard many estimates of how much you should invest in a home, the most frequent admonition being, "Do not pay more than two or two and one-half times your annual gross income." In some instances this may be good advice, but should you spend two times the *total* family income? Or two times the annual income *after* income taxes have been deducted? When should it be two times and when two and one-half times income? Actually, these estimates are only a few of many factors which you should consider when deciding how much to pay for a home.

RULES OF THUMB

The amount you should pay for a home depends basically on how eager you and your family are to own one. If you look upon a home as merely a place in which to eat, sleep, and change clothes, you should invest much less than if you have always wanted a home and plan to use it as a center for family life. Reports from home financers do show that the purchase prices of homes will range from as high as three and one-half to as low as one times the total annual income earned by the principal family wage earner, disregarding deductions of any type. For example, if the principal wage earner receives a total gross annual income of $8,000 before salary deductions, then the family could afford a home costing between $18,000 and $24,000. The majority of such families will probably buy a home costing between $16,000 (two times) and $20,000 (two and one-half times income). In fact, many mortgage lenders will use this type of calculation as a first means of deciding whether you are making the kind of home purchase that they wish to finance. In any case, the price will tend to be a greater multiple of your income if your income is low.

The amount to invest in a home may also be calculated as a percentage of your monthly income either before or after federal income taxes have been deducted. Usually, it is assumed that the total housing payments each month for mortgage interest and principal, property taxes, property insurance, and minimal allowance for necessary utilities should not exceed 20 to 25 per cent of the monthly income of the principal wage earner after the deduction of federal income taxes (nor more than 25 per cent of the income before these taxes are deducted). For example, a family with principal monthly income before taxes of $700 ($8,400 yearly) should not pay more for their housing than $175 monthly ($700 × 25%). However, the typical family usually spends between 15 and 25 per cent of its monthly income for housing. This, of course, says nothing about the price of the house, which is left to your bargaining powers and shopping abilities.

WHAT DO YOU WANT?

You can afford to pay more than the standards usually suggested if, as indicated previously, you are very interested in securing a family home and have prepared for its purchase. This means that you should already have purchased and paid for almost all of the furniture and appliances which you feel you will need for the home; that you have not obligated yourself heavily for the purchase of a car, clothing, or other personal goods; and, the total size of your family is not so large that its care takes a major portion of your income. You may also plan to pay more than the average family if the principal wage earner has been regularly employed, has received regular job promotions and salary increases, and has a position which promises more of these. Younger families, for example, in which the principal wage earner is just starting up the salary ladder can often plan to pay more than the older family in which the wage earner is in a stabilized job situation.

You may be able to pay more for a home if you have trained yourself and your family in good financial habits. For instance, you can afford a more expensive home if you have been able to put even a small amount in a savings account regularly; if you have purchased life insurance through regular payments; and if you have purchased personal property such as an automobile, furniture, or appliances without obligating yourself to excessive monthly payments, and if you have paid each installment as it became due. Furthermore, if you do buy a home, you will find that having a savings account, or life insurance with a cash value, provides a reserve which can be used to continue house payments if family income should be temporarily interrupted for any reason.

LOOK CAREFULLY AT THE HOME

The amount which you should pay for a home will also depend upon whether the home is old or new, large or small, expensive or cheap, whether appliances are built into the home, and the general condition of the home. The larger, newer, more expensively equipped and built homes will have higher purchase prices and cost more to maintain. However, in the long run it may be cheaper to purchase a newer home that is already equipped with most major appliances such as stoves, ovens, refrigerators, dish- and clothes-washing machines, and air conditioning. Great care and planning should precede the purchase of an older home that you plan to modernize because the costs of modernization may often exceed the value of the home and amount to more than what you may have planned for.

> *A Basic Principle:* What you *can* pay for a home depends largely upon you. What you *must* pay depends upon the kind of home you buy and the neighborhood and city in which it is located.
>
> *Lender's Rules of Thumb:* The house price should not exceed 2 to 2.5 times gross family income. Regarding monthly payments:

1. All costs of owning (financing and operating) should not exceed 20 to 25 per cent of gross monthly family income, or;
2. All costs of owning should not exceed 20 per cent of the gross family take-home pay, or;
3. Minimum costs of home ownership (loan payment, property taxes, property insurance, and minimum maintenance) should not exceed the gross family income divided by 60.

DOWN PAYMENT AND LOAN TERMS

First-time buyers are always concerned about how much down payment they should make and what kinds of loan terms they should seek. Presumably, the larger the down payment, the lower the monthly loan payment. On the other hand, the larger down payment denies the family cash that they might want to use for redecorating, for new furniture, or for other items. Unfortunately, home loans are not intended to cover the costs of such items. Even if the family had nothing it wished to buy, it might want to keep a cash reserve earning interest in a savings account.

Given the expectations of most families that their incomes will be rising along with home prices, more and more of them are asking only what the monthly payment may be. They do not concern themselves with either the length of loan repayment or the interest rate. Generally, these families assume that they will be selling the home long before they pay off the loan and will make a profit through price increases. This is in distinct contrast to the philosophy of earlier years that home-buyers should be worried about the length of the loan and the rate of interest. This concern stemmed from the realization that a 40-year loan at a high rate of interest could produce interest payments over the entire life of the loan equal to 2 or 3 times the original purchase price of the home. There are no rules about this and you will have to decide for yourself on this. Later, I discuss the consequences of picking particular loan terms.

FINANCIAL CHECKLISTS

There are four kinds of financial analyses you will want to make before you decide how much to pay for your home and how much you can afford to pay to operate it:

Before you complete the purchase there are some items you will want to check (Table 2-1). Basically, the financial concerns include total price you will pay, cash needed for down payment, sources of the loan you will need and its terms, size of monthly loan payment, added costs connected with the change of ownership, and additional costs of furnishing the home in order to make it immediately liveable.

All of these items are subject to negotiation between you as a buyer, the home seller, and the home lender. The amounts will vary considerably among sellers and lenders, so do some shopping before you settle on the final terms.

There are many kinds of costs connected with the change of ownership of a home, and these tend to vary from area to area (Table 2-2). Only rarely does a law require that a buyer or a seller pay a particular cost. On the other hand, there is usually a strong tradition about which costs buyers and sellers pay independently and what they share. You may find that a lawyer is useful in helping you negotiate the costs. On the other hand, you may wish to bargain yourself so we have listed names of items which can become costs. I suggest that you or your representative use the exhibit as a guide to decide what has to be paid, what the amounts will be and who pays each.

Pay particular attention to the lower portion of the table. Normally, you should ask that any of these items be completed before you move in and before you make the last payments on the purchase. You will find that you may ask for a reduced price equal to your estimates of the costs of completing these items, but that you will probably pay more than this when you finally get around to doing them. You may wish to avoid the annoyance of undertaking these items and agree to a higher price if the seller will do the work.

Table 2-1   Can I Afford to Buy This Home?
What are the Financial Terms?

Have complete answers to all of the following questions:
1. Date on which the house can be occupied   _____
2. Total purchase price of the house   _____
3. Cash down payment required   _____
4. Date by which down payment must be made   _____
5. Amount of money to be secured from a first loan   _____
6. From whom can the loan be secured   _____
7. What will be the interest rate and years of the loan   _____
8. Size of monthly payments: total amount   _____
        Amounts applied to: Loan_____
                             Taxes_____   Insurance _____
9. Amount of money to be secured from a second loan
10. From whom can the second loan be secured
11. What will be the interest rate and years of the second loan
12. Size of monthly payments for second loan
13. Are there any impounds and what will be the costs
    (Impounds: An amount set aside monthly to pay property taxes, property insurance when due)
14. Costs of all items of furniture and equipment to be purchased with the house:
        Item_____Cost_____Item_____Cost_____
        Item_____Cost_____Item_____Cost_____
        Item_____Cost_____Item_____Cost_____

Table 2-2   What Should I Ask the Seller?

How much of the following will the seller pay? These answers will help you determine how much cash over the down payment. These are the hidden costs.

	Buyer	Seller
Real estate broker's commission		
Costs of securing the loan		
Costs of legal advice in preparing papers to transfer property		
Title insurance or proof of title		
Preparation of deed of title and recording		
Notary fees for recorded instruments		
Survey of property lines		
Property appraisal fees		
Taxes and assessments now due		
Loan prepayment penalties		
Insurance premiums due		
Termite and dry rot inspection		
Closing costs (layer or escrow)		
Other: _____		

Are any of the following items to be completed before the new owner moves in and who pays for them:

DESCRIPTION			COST
	BUYER	SELLER	
Repairs: _____			
Painting: _____			
Decorating: _____			
Alterations: _____			
Other: _____			

The best way to determine these costs is to ask the previous owner to show you the bills. On the other hand, you can develop your own estimates by checking with utility companies, insurance companies, home service companies, and appropriate departments in city hall. Some costs are clearly related to your own ideas of how a home should be maintained. If painting, repairs, decorating, or alterations are postponed or not done on a regular basis, the home will slowly deteriorate and lose value. In fact, most American homes are under-maintained, which explains why these particular costs may not equal more than 1 or 2 per cent of the current market value of the home.

The costs can rise rapidly if you buy some of the many kinds of services available to you. Some services include periodic treatment for insects, lawn care, water-softener servicing, landscaping (tree trim-ming, gardening, etc.), and trash and garbage pickup. In each case, be sure to read your contract for services carefully so that you understand clearly what you are paying for. Sometimes there are little extras that seem reasonable but which can add up to a considerable bill at the end of the year.

In all maintenance undertakings, be sure to use a written contract and be sure that materials and work are clearly specified. You might want a lawyer to advise you on the contract. You will find that your local mortgage-loan officer can be very helpful in determining whether the contract for the services is properly drawn and protects your rights. In subsequent chapters, I offer some suggestions about dealing with contractors.

Table 2-3   How Much Does It Cost to Operate the Home?

What are the yearly costs of the following items:	Annual Cost
Heating	_____
Water heating	_____
Water costs	_____
Gas for cooking	_____
Electricity	_____
Lawn care, including landscaping	_____
Garbage and trash disposal	_____
Property taxes	_____
Special assessments	_____
Water softener service	_____
Property, liability, fire, theft insurance	_____

Maintenance costs:

Painting (Exterior _____   _____
          interior)

Table 2-3   *(cont.)*

Repairs
Decorating
Alterations
Other

Monthly financing payment   First mortgage _____
                                                    Second mortgage _____
                            Total housing expenses   _____

                            Your total family income
                            before taxes and deductions   _____

                            Housing expenses/income   _____

If the total of these items seems too high, perhaps you should check them again to see
if any can be cut. If this seems impossible, (and remember, they will probably go up),
perhaps you should shop for a less costly home or try to get your monthly loan payment
lowered. If, after all of this, the amounts are too high, you might consider waiting a bit
and accumulating a larger down payment or buying a less expensive home.

If you have persevered to this point and still feel you can afford
the home you want to buy, you still have one final financial analysis.
Table 2-4 represents a composite of the kinds of items you will have to
complete when seeking a home loan. Basically, the lender wants to
know: (1) if you have had experience in buying on credit and have
managed to accumulate some property in this way (what do I own?);
(2) if you have so many current debts that you cannot afford to pay 20
to 30 per cent more of your income to own and operate the home (what
do I owe?); and (3) if you have a net financial balance that will permit
you to pay all of the costs calculated (in Tables 2-1, 2-2, and 2-3) and
also make your monthly loan payments. Further, the lender will want
to know if you have some form of asset or cash reserve that would
allow you to continue your monthly payments for at least 6 months if
your earned income should be interrupted.

In calculating the total family income, you can include your
spouse's earnings as well as earnings from other investments in estimating your total gross family income. Usually overtime pay, special
bonuses or cash awards are not given full weight in determining your
ability to pay, even if you have been receiving them regularly. Lenders

do want to make loans to qualified borrowers, so be sure to provide all of the financial information you have.

Lenders will not mind your visiting them before you apply for a loan and discussing with you how they make their analyses and what kinds of information they expect you to furnish. You will find lenders vary in their standards for borrowers, so be sure to shop around and get the best terms available.

Table 2-4   The Prospective Home Buyers' Financial Analysis Sheet

When you ask for a home loan most lenders will ask you the kinds of questions we list here. They want to know if you have good savings habits (what you own) and whether you have already committed yourself to too much borrowing already (what you owe).

Present Dollar Value

What Do I Own?

Personal property: Furniture and other furnishings for the home $_____
　　　　　　　　　　Clothing for the family   _____
　　　　　　　　　　Appliances for the home (radio, tv, clothes,
　　　　　　　　　　　washer and dryer, dishwasher, air conditioning)   _____
　　　　　　　　　　Amount of personal loan not paid _____

Automobile: Make_____ Year_____ Mileage_____
　　　　　　　Amount owed on auto loan _____

Life insurance in force: Amount $_____Cash value $_____
　　　　　　　Loans on insurance_____ Beneficiary_____

Securities owned:_____ Type_____ Face value_____

　　　　　　　　_____   _____
　　　　　　　　_____   _____
　　　　　　　　_____   _____

Real estate owned: Type_____
　　　　　　　　　　Market value_____ less unpaid loans_____

Business(es) owned: Type_____ for (years)_____

Other assets: (including savings accounts) _____$ _____
　　　　　　　_____$ _____
　　　　　　　_____$ _____

Total Present Dollar Value of all Assets Owned $_____

Total Still Due

What Do I Owe?

Installment payments:
　　Kind   Original amount Total unpaid Monthly payment
　Automobile   _____
　Furniture   _____

Table 2-4 *(cont.)*

Appliances	_____		
Medical expenses	_____		
Life insurance	_____		
Other: _____	_____		
	_____		
Totals	$_____	$ _____	$ _____

My Net Financial Position at the End of the Year

Income:

Salary (gross before deduction)	$_____	Expenses:		
Salary (after deductions, your		All loan pymts		
take-home pay)	_____	Living expenses		
		Food _____		
Earnings from:				
Securities	_____	Clothing _____		
Properties	_____	Transportation _____	_____	
Interest on savings accts	_____	Property upkeep:		_____
Business	_____	Other: _____		
Over-time, extra jobs	_____	(utilities) _____		
	_____	(rent) _____		
Other income from members of				
the immediate family	_____	_____		_____
Total income (annually)	$_____	Total expenses	$_____	
Net Dollar Amount Available Annually for All Housing Costs			$_____	

Finally: Any obligations such as being a guarantor on a note or loan; or as
the result of law suits, judgments, should be deducted.

HOW MUCH SHOULD YOU PAY?

||||||||||||||||||||||||||||||||||||||||||||||||||||||||||||||||||||||||||||||||||||||||||||||||||||||||||||||||||||||||||||||||||||||||

3

   Establishing the price you should pay for the home you select is a process of negotiation since the price you pay may be 10 to 15 per cent less than what the seller asks. This happens because many sellers, and the real estate brokers working for them, expect buyers to want to negotiate for lower prices. Actually the determination of the sales is difficult because it is usually set by comparison with the prices obtained for other similar kinds of homes, and really represents only an "informed" guess as to what the price should be.

   Other reasons why the price you pay may be less than the price asked by the seller include:

   1. The house is not selling and the seller must have the money.

2. The available financing will require too large a down payment by buyers.
3. There are too many repairs and improvements to be made before the house is liveable.
4. Too many houses of this type are being offered for sale.

On the other hand, the price may be firm because the seller and broker have made a careful study of the market and know what "the price is right." Real estate markets do change, however, and houses of the type you are interested may be in short supply with many buyers searching for just this type of house. Perhaps the most important reason why the price cannot be lowered is because a very favorable mortgage, (that is, one with a low interest rate or a high-value loan which requires a very small down payment), is available.

How then do you make sure that you are paying the "right price?"

ASSISTANCE TO YOU
IN SETTING THE PURCHASE PRICE

There are many ways in which you can determine the purchase price, ranging from those that will cost money to those that will cost you time.

Appraisers

If you look in the yellow pages of the phone book, you will find lists of appraisers who will establish a proper market price and furnish you with a written statement of their estimate. You might also ask the mortgage lending officers in your local banks or savings and loan associations or local real estate brokers for someone they would recommend.

An appraiser will charge. How much so will depend upon how

elaborate a report you ask to be prepared. Time is required to make the analysis. Prices can range from minimums of $25 or $50 to $300 or more. The time can range from one or two days or weeks depending upon how busy the appraiser may be.

Inspection Services

The price you pay should be related to the amount of money you may have to spend to make the home a liveable place for your family. Again, reference to the phone book or local home lenders can help you locate persons or firms who will inspect the house—plumbing, electrical systems, interior and exterior repairs, roof, painting, and mechanical equipment, such as water heaters, which come with the home—and give you a statement of the condition of the home and what it might cost to improve, according to the standards you feel are necessary or ones that are necessary to meet local building code requirements.

Some real estate offices will now offer home-improvement insurance that protects you against the costs of any needed repairs during the life of the policy, usually about one year. You should ask about this.

How much money and time? Again, both vary, but will probably equal the costs of the appraisal. Incidentally, some appraisers do include comments on needed repairs in their appraisal reports. Perhaps you could ask for this to be included.

Real Estate Brokers

Real estate brokers are usually hired and paid by sellers. For this reason, they will tend to protect the sellers' interests in any negotiations about price. Some may suggest that perhaps the seller would lower the price if you really are a serious buyer, but usually this is anticipated and the price is set so that it can be lowered. Legally, brokers must tell you the truth about any defects which might cause you not to buy the house, but they are not required to volunteer information which might injure their client's interests.

Can you hire a broker to help you set a price? Usually not,

because they cannot make a "fair" profit for themselves by doing this as compared to selling homes. Perhaps you might pay a broker to represent you in the negotiation for the price. Brokers rarely sell their services to buyers, but if you find a broker whom you like particularly well, it would not hurt to ask for assistance—at a price.

You Can Tour and Compare

Perhaps the best way for you to get a reasonable notion of the prices being asked for homes is to tour areas in which you would like to live and homes you might be willing to buy. In each case, you can ask about the terms of sale and may even be able to determine whether the price will be cut. If you spend about a week visiting 10 to 20 homes, any one of which you might be willing to buy, you will be reasonably "expert" in deciding what you should pay.

TRADEOFFS IN SETTING THE PURCHASE PRICE

You will find that probably you cannot find the home that exactly meets your needs—the location may be wrong, the house too old or too new (expensive), too big or too little. These are some guidelines to help you decide how to tradeoff these items.

Good House, Poor Location.   The house is ideal in every way, but the neighborhood is bad. Perhaps homes are not maintained, traffic is heavy, private homes are changing to apartment houses or other different kinds of uses. Since you can do little to change adverse trends in a neighborhood, you probably should not buy. However, if the house is irresistible, negotiate carefully for the lowest possible price and anticipate that you may want to move before too long.

Poor House, Good Location.   Find out whether you can have the house renovated to meet your needs and your pocketbook. In any case, get a firm estimate of all outlays and make sure that when their total is added to the purchase price, the total does not exceed the "fair market value" of the house.

Big or Little. The costs of owning and operating homes is rising sharply and are expected to continue to rise. This is one case where, if your family living style can help, small can be beautiful.

Old or New. Older homes needing "fixup" can be real headaches. Not even expert builders or contractors can give you a firm estimate of what renovating or improving may cost. Whatever you receive as an estimate add about 10 to 20 per cent. Preferably, you should buy the older home that is already improved. That way you know the costs and what the home looks like. Homes approaching 20 to 30 years old may require substantial improvements in such basics as plumbing, heating, and equipment.

Market Conditions. Before you buy you should visit other homes for sale and visit with selling brokers to determine whether buyers exceed sellers or the reverse. If you are in an area in which there are many buyers and only a few homes, you will find that negotiating for a better price is difficult. In such cases, you may want to offer the seller a down payment to hold the home until you can determine whether you want to pay the price asked and what terms you might want to add. You may lose the down payment if you do not buy, but you may save yourself money in the long run. If there are fewer buyers and sellers, then you can negotiate. Don't rush; use the experts. Make sure that you get your money's worth.

THE PROCESS OF PRICE NEGOTIATION

Can you negotiate for a better price? Yes, in almost all circumstances. The first step, however, is for you to determine what you are willing to pay, price and down payment, and what you want the seller to do. When you make your first offer, keep it at the lowest possible level. If met with a refusal wait and contact the seller later, outlining what you might be willing to do in return for certain actions on the seller's part. If you are dealing through a broker, remember that the broker is paid to get the best price and terms and is paid according to the price obtained. On the other hand, if you can convince the seller and the broker that you are a serious buyer, well informed about the market and the house you want, you will find you can negotiate for more favorable terms.

What are some ways of negotiating?

1. Present a list of repairs or improvements and what you think they would cost.
2. Compare the price to the prices of similar homes you have visited.
3. Submit an appraisal report which supports your price.
4. Offer a higher down payment.
5. Discuss other homes that you can buy.
6. Bring along an expert, perhaps another broker, who can talk about prices, repairs, terms.
7. Do not rush into buying, but indicate your willingness to continue price negotiations.
8. Let the selling broker take a small commission.
9. Make a ridiculously small offer the first time—surprisingly, this works occasionally—but do not close the door to further negotiations.
10. Keep your early price offers about 10 to 20 per cent below the price, if this includes your estimates of improvement costs.
11. Never accept a seller's statement that the price is "firm."
12. Don't panic; hold onto what you think is the right price. There are other homes you can buy. If sellers have been trying to sell for some time, they will negotiate. Keep an eye open for new homes offered for sale by a builder. Usually builders will take lower prices because they must get their money out of the homes so they can build others.

USE AN ORGANIZED APPROACH TO SETTING PRICE

Finally, I offer some tables that may help you set the price. Before discussing them, however, let's review the steps in an organized approach to finding a home and setting a price.

1. Use classified advertising to determine the locations in which homes of the kind you want are offered for sale.

2. Use a map to lay out your visit to the areas in which you may wish to buy, using the neighborhood checklist included in this book. Visit any homes which are open for inspection (usually this is on weekends).

3. Identify broker offices which are offering homes for sale. Visit them and discuss the market and house prices.

4. Narrow your choices to at least two, but not more than three, homes and follow our suggestions on estimating prices.

Your Appraisal

Table 3-1 provides a checklist you can use to keep track of the homes about which you are getting serious. Of particular importance are the reasons given by sellers for wanting to sell. You can judge which reasons are really important, for example, moving to a new job, family breakup, or another home already built or purchased. You should determine maximum and minimum price potentials as indications of the range within which you set your price.

Finally, put your price on each of the homes in which you are interested and the reasons why you prefer that home at that price. You should then be able to decide on which home you will make an offer and what your minimum terms will be.

Table 3-1   What Should This Home Sell for As Compared to Other Homes in the Neighborhood?

One of the most effective means of deciding how much you should pay for a home is to compare it with other homes in the neighborhood which have been sold recently. The following check list indicates the kinds of items which are most likely to affect the sales price of a home. You can get information about these from persons who have recently purchased homes or from local real estate offices. There is no way in which you can get an easy answer as to what you should pay even after you have collected all of the information. You must decide for yourself what you think you would want to pay after you have seen what other persons have paid for homes.

	Home I Am Planning to Buy	*Comparable Properties*		
Comparison factor		*A*	*B*	*C*
1. Address	_____	_____	_____	_____

Table 3-1 *(cont.)*

Comparison factor	Home I Am Planning to Buy	Comparable Properties		
		A	B	C
2. Quality (see neighborhood checklist)	_____	_____	_____	_____
3. Lot size (sq. ft.) (length × width)	_____	_____	_____	_____
4. Architectural style	_____	_____	_____	_____
5. Room count total/bedrooms/baths	_____	_____	_____	_____
6. Age of house (in years)	_____	_____	_____	_____
7. Costs of all repairs you think should be made	_____	_____	_____	_____
8. Terms of sale	_____	_____	_____	_____
Date	_____	_____	_____	_____
Down payment	_____	_____	_____	_____
Size of first loan (total/amount not yet paid)	_____	_____	_____	_____
Remaining years	_____	_____	_____	_____
Interest rate	_____	_____	_____	_____
Size of second loan	_____	_____	_____	_____
Remaining years	_____	_____	_____	_____
Interest rate	_____	_____	_____	_____
9. Reasons for sale	_____	_____	_____	_____
10. Actual price paid vs. asking price	_____	_____	_____	_____
11. Other factors:	_____	_____	_____	_____

1998389

Table 3-1 *(cont.)*

Sales of typical properties in the neighborhood:

Range: from $ _____ to $ _____
Average sales price $ _____

Estimated Value of the Home You are Considering:

As compared to:

Property A the home is worth $ _____ because _____

Property B the home is worth $ _____ because _____

Property C the home is worth $ _____ because _____

Your offering price is $ _____ because:

HOW TO USE THE MORTGAGE PAYMENT TABLE

The following table shows the monthly payment that would have to be made each month for each $1,000 borrowed at a given rate of interest for a given period of years.

For example:

1. I have borrowed $10,000 with which to buy a home and I agree to pay 6 per cent interest for 20 years.

   From the table I obtain the figure $7.17 which I multiply by 10 (10,000 ÷ 1,000). The answer, $71.70, is the amount I must pay monthly to repay the 6 per cent loan in 20 years.

   If I multiply the $71.70 by 12, the answer $860.40 is the amount I will pay on the loan annually.

   If I multiply $860.40 by 20 the answer $17,208 is the total amount of money I will repay to the lender for lending me $10,000 for 20 years at 6 per cent interest. The $7,208 over the $10,000 which I borrowed represents the cost to me of using the lender's money.

2. Suppose that I have borrowed $1,000 for 20 years at 6.5 per cent interest. The table does not have 6.5 per cent interest figures.

   The figure for 7 per cent for 20 years is $7.76

Table 3-2 Monthly Payment per $1,000 of Loan Needed to Amortize the Loan[1]

	Interest Rate (in per cent)									
No. of Years	1	2	3	4	5	6	7	8	9	10
1	83.79	84.24	84.69	85.15	85.61	86.01		86.99	87.45	87.92
2	42.10	42.54	42.99	43.43	43.88	44.33	44.78	45.23	45.68	46.14
3	28.21	28.64	29.09	29.53	29.98	30.43	30.88	31.34	31.80	32.27
4	21.26	21.70	22.14	22.58	23.03	23.49	23.95	24.41	24.89	25.36
5	17.09	17.53	17.97	18.42	18.88	19.34	19.81	20.28	20.76	21.25
6	14.32	14.75	15.20	15.65	16.11	16.58	17.05	17.53	18.03	18.53
7	12.34	12.77	13.22	13.67	14.14	14.61	15.10	15.59	16.09	16.60
8	10.84	11.28	11.73	12.19	12.66	13.15	13.64	14.14	14.65	15.17
9	9.69	10.13	10.58	11.05	11.52	12.01	12.51	13.02	13.54	14.08
10	8.76	9.20	9.66	10.13	10.61	11.11	11.62	12.13	12.67	13.22
11	8.00	8.45	8.91	9.38	9.87	10.37	10.89	11.42	11.96	12.52
12	7.37	7.82	8.28	8.76	9.25	9.76	10.29	10.82	11.38	11.95
13	6.84	7.28	7.75	8.24	8.74	9.25	9.79	10.33	10.90	11.48
14	6.38	6.83	7.30	7.79	8.29	8.82	9.36	9.91	10.49	11.08
15	5.98	6.44	6.91	7.40	7.91	8.44	8.99	9.56	10.14	10.75
16	5.64	6.01	6.57	7.06	7.58	8.12	8.63	9.25	9.85	10.46
17	5.33	5.79	6.27	6.77	7.29	7.84	8.40	8.98	9.59	10.21
18	5.06	5.52	6.00	6.51	7.04	7.59	8.16	8.75	9.36	10.00
19	4.82	5.28	5.76	6.27	6.81	7.37	7.95	8.55	9.17	9.81
20	4.60	5.01	5.55	6.06	6.60	7.17	7.76	8.36	9.00	9.65

Table 3-2 Monthly Payment per $1,000 of Loan Needed to Amortize the Loan[1] (cont.)

No. of Years	Interest Rate (in per cent)									
	1	2	3	4	5	6	7	8	9	10
21	4.40	4.86	5.36	5.88	6.42	6.99	7.59	8.20	8.85	9.51
22	4.22	4.69	5.18	5.71	6.26	6.84	7.44	8.06	8.71	9.38
23	4.01	4.52	5.03	5.55	6.11	6.69	7.30	7.93	8.59	9.27
24	3.91	4.37	4.88	5.41	5.97	6.56	7.18	7.82	8.49	9.17
25	3.77	4.24	4.75	5.28	5.85	6.45	7.07	7.72	8.39	9.09
26	3.64	4.11	4.62	5.17	5.74	6.34	6.97	7.63	8.31	9.01
27	3.52	4.00	4.51	5.06	5.64	6.24	6.88	7.54	8.23	8.94
28	3.41	3.89	4.41	4.96	5.54	6.16	6.80	7.47	8.16	8.88
29	3.31	3.79	4.31	4.86	5.45	6.08	6.73	7.40	8.10	8.82
30	3.22	3.70	4.22	4.78	5.37	6.00	6.66	7.34	8.05	8.78

[1]This table is based on the assumption that the final payment would differ from preceding payments because it would be used to make up deficiencies caused by rounding to nearest cent.

The figure for 6 per cent for 20 years is	7.17
The difference between the figures	.59

If I multiply .59 × .5, the answer is .295
If I add .295 to $7.17 (the smaller amount) the answer of $7.47 (rounded to the nearest cent) is the amount I pay monthly at 6.5 per cent interest for 20 years.

3. Suppose that I have borrowed $12,225 at 6.6 per cent interest for 20 years.

The figure for 7 per cent for 20 years is	$7.76
The figure for 6 per cent for 20 years is	7.17
The difference between the figures	.59

If I multiply .59 × .6 per cent the answer is .354
If I add .354 to the lower of the 2 figures above ($7.17 + .354) the answer is $7.524, the amount I pay monthly for each $1,000. If I multiply $7.524 × 12.225 ($12,225 ÷ 1,000) the answer of $91.98 is the monthly mortgage payment which I must make.

FINANCING AND PRICE

The financial matter that will be of most concern to you apart from the price will be the monthly mortgage payment. Usually any home you buy will include a mortgage with a known mortgage payment. However, you may want to use Table 3-2 ahead of time to help you in your negotiations. For example, the monthly payment per $1,000 of loan for a 9 per cent loan of 15 years is $10.41, and for 30 years the amount is $8.05. Perhaps this difference would reduce your monthly home ownership costs so that you could pay a little more.

An important reason for understanding how to affect your monthly payments is that if you can secure a larger down payment so that only one loan is needed to buy the home, you may get a lower price. Equally important, if you must secure a loan at a higher interest rate, you should determine the additional cost this would entail in order to extend the terms of the mortgage, thereby reducing the monthly payments to the amount you can afford to pay.

Notice that increasing the interest rate from 4 to 8 per cent adds about 30 per cent to the loan payment for a 15 year loan. On the other hand, reducing an 8 per cent loan from 30 years to 15 years swells the payment by about the same amount. In other words, you can trade off interest amounts and terms without changing your percentage of increase in payments. The real impact is in the dollar amount. Be prepared to negotiate on both interest rate and term, but you will have more success in getting longer terms than lower rates.

One of the basic principles of mortgage-loan borrowing is that when you make a monthly payment, any interest owed is paid for from your first payment, and anything left is used to reduce that amount that you owe. Table 3-3 contains an illustration of how a monthly payment would be allocated each month to interest and principal. Notice that for total payments on this loan for 5 years of $15,448.80, the principal has been reduced by only $1,318.36. In effect, the price of the home has been increased by the amount of the interest payment, $14,130.04. Fortunately, you can deduct interest payments from your reportable, taxable income so that your financial position is somewhat better than indicated.

Most families concern themselves only with the actual monthly payment and do not worry about the impact of interest. On the other hand, if you obtain a $20,000 loan for 30 years at 9 per cent, your total payments would be $57,960, of which $37,960 would represent interest, or an actual increase in your home price.

Now that I have introduced the problems of mortgage financing, in Chapter 4 I can offer suggestions on how to find a lender and to negotiate for the best possible loan terms.

**Table 3-3   Allocation of Mortgage Monthly Payments
To Principal and Interest
($32,000 loan, 9 per cent interest, thirty years)**

Mos.	Payment	Interest	Principal	Balance
1	$257.48	$240.00	$17.48	$31,982.56
2		239.87	17.61	31,964.91
3		239.74	17.74	31,947.17
4		239.60	17.88	31,929.29
5		239.47	18.01	31,911.28
6		239.33	18.15	31,893.13

Table 3-3 *(cont.)*

Mos.	Payment	Interest	Principal	Balance		
7		239.20	18.28	31,874.84		
8		239.06	18.42	31,856.43		
9		238.92	18.56	31,837.87		
10		238.78	18.70	31,819.17		
11		238.64	18.84	31,800.34		
12		238.50	18.98	31,781.36	2,871.11	218.65
13		238.36	19.12	31,762.24		
14		238.22	19.26	31,742.98		
15		238.07	19.41	31,723.57		
16		237.93	19.55	31,704.02		
17		237.78	19.70	31,684.32		
18		237.63	19.85	31,664.47		
19		237.48	20.00	31,644.47		
20		237.33	20.15	31,624.33		
21		237.18	20.33	31,604.03		
22		237.03	20.45	31,583.58		
23		236.88	20.60	31,562.98		
24		236.72	20.76	31,542.22	2,850.58	239.18
25		236.57	20.91	31,521.30		
26		236.41	21.07	31,500.23		
27		236.25	21.23	31,479.00		
28		236.09	21.39	31,457.61		
29		235.93	21.55	31,436.07		
30		235.77	21.71	31,414.36		
31		235.61	21.87	31,392.49		
32		235.44	22.04	31,370.45		
33		235.28	22.20	31,348.25		
34		235.11	22.37	31,325.88		
35		234.94	22.54	31,303.35		
36		234.78	22.70	31,280.64	2,828.18	261.58
37		234.60	22.88	31,257.77		
38		234.43	23.05	31,234.72		
39		234.26	23.22	31,211.50		
40		234.09	23.39	31,188.11		
41		233.91	23.57	31,164.54		
42		233.73	23.75	31,140.79		
43		233.56	23.92	31,116.87		
44		233.38	24.10	31,092.77		
45		233.20	24.28	31,068.48		
46		233.01	24.47	31,044.02		
47		232.83	24.65	31,019.37		
48		232.65	24.83	30,994.53	2,803.65	286.11

Table 3-3 *(cont.)*

Mos.	Payment	Interest	Principal	Balance		
49		232.46	25.02	30,969.51		
50		232.27	25.21	30,944.30		
51		232.08	25.40	30,918.90		
52		231.89	25.59	30,893.31		
53		231.70	25.78	30,867.53		
54	'	231.51	25.97	30,841.56		
55		231.31	26.17	30,815.39		
56		231.12	26.36	30,789.03		
57		230.92	26.56	30,762.46		
58		230.72	26.76	30,735.70		
59		230.52	26.96	30,708.74		
60		230.32	27.16	30,681.57	2,776.82	312.94
					$14,130.34	$1,318.46

HOW DO YOU FINANCE THE PURCHASE?

||||||||||||||||||||||||||||||||||||||||||||||||||||||||||||||||||||||||||||||||||||||||||||||||||||||||||||||||

4

When you are ready to purchase the home which you have selected, you will probably find that you will not have enough cash to pay for more than 25 per cent of the purchase price and, if you are like most American families, you will prefer to pay not more than 10 per cent down. For example, U.S. Bureau of the Census figures show that at least 80 per cent of all homes are purchased with the assistance of some type of loan. Normally, you will secure the additional funds by borrowing from a commercial bank, a savings bank, a savings and loan association, or an insurance company, each of which will have a variety of financing plans to offer you. They will usually agree to lend the money if you will agree to pay back the original amount that you borrow plus interest on what you have not repaid in monthly installments, and if you pledge the house as security for repayment of the loan. The pledging of the house as security is accomplished by means of a mortgage or deed of trust which means that if you fail to make your payments according to the loan terms, the lender can have your house sold publicly and apply the proceeds on the amounts owed. First I shall discuss the kinds of terms which the lenders usually offer to prospective home buyers, and then the kinds of mortgages which are available and the kinds of terms to which you must usually agree.

SAVINGS AND LOAN ASSOCIATIONS

Savings and loan associations are financial institutions chartered by either state or federal agencies primarily for the purpose of collecting savings in local communities and then making these funds available locally for the purchase of single-family homes, although they do provide a limited amount of financing for other types of property purchases. The principal difference between a federally chartered and a state-chartered association is that state-chartered associations can sometimes make loans on more different types of properties than federally chartered associations, and they may be able to be slightly more liberal in their lending terms.

The typical savings and loan association, because it specializes in home loans, can make relatively large loans for relatively long terms. That is, it can make a loan which represents a relatively high percentage of the total purchase price, often up to 80 per cent of what you pay for the home, and can give you up to 20, or in exceptional cases, to 30 years in which to repay your loan. This type of loan is known as a conventional loan since the repayment of the loan is not guaranteed nor insured by any governmental agency and it can be made by any type of lending institution. The amount of the purchase price which can be financed and the terms on which the money is to be repaid are determined by the charter provisions of the association, which are the same for all federally chartered associations but differ for the state-chartered associations. As long as the associations do not exceed the loan-to-value ratios and terms set forth in their charters, they may introduce any modifications they feel are proper. This means that you will find different lending terms being offered to you even by savings and loan associations in your local community.

Savings and loan associations not only make loans for the purchase of a home, but also for home repairs and improvements. They do not make loans for the purchase of personal property so that you cannot finance the purchase of an automobile, furniture, or a trip with a loan from a savings and loan association.

Commercial Banks

Commercial banks are also chartered by either federal or state agencies for the purpose of collecting local savings, but primarily to make loans to businessmen, although the making of home loans is usually an important part of their total business. The difference between the federally chartered and the state-chartered associations is about like that between federally and state-chartered savings and loan associations. For example, many state-chartered banks can make loans with only land offered as security for loans, whereas the federally chartered banks cannot.

The mortgage loans which commercial banks make are usually a smaller percentage of the purchase price, usually between 60 and 70 per cent, and for shorter periods of time, usually 15 years, than are the loans from savings and loan associations. In addition, commercial banks are often more selective in making home loans because they prefer to lend money on nonresidential properties or for business purposes. You will probably secure the best bank terms if you seek a home loan from the bank with which you have been making deposits or doing other business. The advantage of using a bank is that it can make all types of personal and business loans, so that it provides a "one stop" financial service.

SAVINGS BANKS

Savings banks are found in the New England and East Coast states and are more like savings and loan associations than commercial banks. They also specialize in home loans with terms closely similar to those of savings and loan associations, although they do make more of the other type loans than the associations.

Insurance Companies

Insurance companies make loans through agents, but all loans must be approved by the company. Because of the manner in which they receive their funds, the insurance companies tend to prefer large loans on business properties or good quality single-family homes. Their loan-to-value ratios are often high, averaging between 60 and 80 per cent of purchase price, and the length of the loans between 20 and 30 years. Their interest rates also tend to be at the low end of the prevailing scale of market rates. They are typically selective in the properties which they will finance, preferring larger, newer properties in well-established neighborhoods.

Insurance companies have developed various types of mortgage insurance plans that they sometimes prefer the borrower to take out, although they may not make it an absolute requirement for obtaining the loan. These insurance policies usually have a term equal to the term of the loan and provide proceeds for paying off the loan if the principal wage earner dies or is incapacitated. Some of the policies also have a cash value that can be used: (1) to pay off the loan before its date of maturity; (2) as an endowment at the end of the loan period; or (3) for monthly payments to the insured or the insured's beneficiaries.

DEALING WITH LENDERS

Securing money for a home mortgage is somewhat akin to shopping for an automobile. There are varieties of financing models to consider; some of them are standard and some can be assembled to meet a special need. For this reason, the prospective borrower should spend some time getting acquainted with the various lenders in the area and determining what kinds of loans they prefer to make and the terms which they usually expect. Table 4-1 is a checklist indicating some of the questions that should be considered before a final decision is made as to which lender with whom to do business.

KINDS OF LOANS

FHA (Federal Housing Administration)

An agency of the federal government (FHA) agrees to reimburse the lender if you fail to pay on your mortgage (trust deed). You pay an insurance premium to the FHA of .5 per cent of the amount borrowed, but the FHA requires that the neighborhood and the house meet minimum standards similar to many suggested in this book. These are long-term, low-down-payment, lower-interest loans.

V.A. (Veterans Administration)

This type of loan is open only to qualified war veterans. The VA performs for the veteran the same services as the FHA; it provides long-term, low-down-payment, low-interest loans at no charge to the veteran.

Conventional

As interest rates and home prices continue to rise, lenders, buyers, and sellers are constantly seeking ways of reducing the periodic, financial burden. As a result, the terms of conventional loans are being changed in many ways. In case you happen to encounter some of these variations, here are their characteristics:

1. *Fixed payment.* The monthly payment on the loan remains the same. Nothing can be changed during the life of the loan—the size of the monthly payment, the interest rate, or the length of the loan.
2. *Variable interest or VRM variable rate mortgage.* The interest rate on your loan may be changed according to a formula which is explained to you at the time you secure the loan. Usually, you must be given six

months' notice of the change, and the total change up and down is limited. You probably have the choice of securing a different loan when a change occurs without having to pay extra to make the change. When the change is made, your monthly payment may stay the same, but the amount credited to principal is reduced so that you will be paying on the loan for a longer time.

3. *Variable term.* The length of the loan may be changed; monthly payments may be changed.

4. *Variable payment.* As the interest rate is changed according to the formula, your monthly payment changes in amount. Another variation keeps the monthly payment in some ratio to your monthly earnings. When you are earning less, your payments are less. As you earn more, you pay more. The net impact of this arrangement is to shorten the term of the loan.

Table 4-1   Estimating the Fees Associated with A Loan

Although all home mortgage lenders may seem to be the same, they differ in many important ways. One of these ways is in the fees which they charge in connection with the process of making a loan. Once you have found a property that you may wish to buy you will find it helpful, and financially sound, to visit more than one lender to get answers to the questions listed below.

Type of Lending Institution

1. What would the lender expect of the house in terms of architecture, age, size, condition, and location to approve a loan?

2. What would determine the amount and terms of the loan. If approved how much would be loaned and for how long?

3. How long would it take to secure the loan?

4. What costs, as indicated below, would be charged for the loan and what would be their amounts?

Item	*(Typical Costs)*	*Dollar Amount*
Escrow fee	($2–10)	
Notary fee	($5–10)	
Loan office fee	(½–1% of loan value)	
Appraisal fee	($25–$300)	
Credit report	($10–20)	
Title policy	($150–250)	
Termite report	($30–$100)	

Table 4-1 *(cont.)*

Item	*(Typical Costs)*	Dollar Amount
Recording fee—mortgage or trust deed	($2–$10)	
Recording fee—deed of title	($2–$10)	
Drawing trust deed or mortgage and note	($25–100)	
Misc. legal fees	($0–$200)	
Fire insurance premium		
Pre-payment penalty		
Loan points	(1–2½% of loan value	
Others: (Tax stamps)	(up to 1% of home price)	

5. What are the limits on the number and amount of mortgage loans which can be made to a particular person?

6. How is the value of the house determined which serves as the basis for establishing the amount of the loan?

7. What is the maximum percentage the lender will loan on the house?

8. What is the maximum term in years?

9. What is the maximum interest rate?

10. Will a first mortgage (or trust deed) be given if the buyer also has to use a second mortgage to pay for the house?

Lending Policies

11. In what areas does the lender prefer to lend?

12. What type of borrower is preferred in terms of: size of loan requested; borrower's income; borrower's occupation?

13. What relation is established between the borrower's income and the amount approved on the loan? (Recall that you may be limited to two to two and one-half times your income.)

14. What is the average size and interest rate on the lender's typical loans?

15. Does the lender make FHA loans? VA loans? Are they being made now?

THE IMPORTANCE
OF TIMING
YOUR PURCHASE

||||||||||||||||||||||||||||||||||||||||||||||||||||||||||||||||||||||||||||||||||||||||||||||||||||||||||||||||||||||||||

5

One of the most important ways of increasing the investment value of the home you purchase is to buy at a lower price in an area which is only now beginning to develop. Growth almost always brings with it increases in home values, particularly if the growth augments the facilities and services which home owners can use. In this chapter I will discuss the nature of the growth of residential areas and the way you can time the purchase of your home to take advantage of a rapid growth potential.

REAL ESTATE WINDFALLS AND WIPEOUTS

A property increases in value when it is attractive and available to many buyers. As the number of buyers increases, property prices will tend to rise. Buyers who see the most home value will bid the highest price. The price paid will then become a standard against which others measure the prices they will pay. The process of growth that increases property use and value potentials is suggested in Figures 5-1 and 5-2.

When the population in a given area begins to increase (Figure 5-1), the potential for higher real estate prices emerges. The first indication that the growth may continue is found when local governments provide public water, followed by the installation of roads, utilities, and sewer connections. Some builders feel that the best indication of a real potential for land-value increases lies in the connection of the sewer systems of individual properties to public disposal systems.

An acceleration of real estate prices becomes a real potential if the early installation of public capital improvements attracts large numbers of people. That is, population usually increases annually at a steady rate of 2 to 3 per cent or more, but public improvements may cause this rate to double or triple. A 3 per cent annual rate means that the population will double every 24 years. (To determine in how many years an amount will double when the annual percentage increase is known, divide 72 by the interest rate.)

Other factors which can be monitored as a measure of the increased price potentials of homes are listed in the figure. Notice that the first indications that prices may not continue to increase is the topping out of a business boom. (Booms are accompanied by increased employment and unemployment rates under 5 per cent). Real estate prices tend to rise rapidly during a business boom and to decline with equal rapidity once the boom begins to slacken. Enthusiasm generated by increasingly better business conditions encourages investors to seek raw land where they believe the next growth will occur. As the potential boom is not realized, or does not amount to as much as was anticipated, land speculators begin to sell out their purchases at prices lower than those they paid. Since most land is purchased with large amounts of financing, many of the land buyers simply quit paying on their lands and let them revert to the lenders. A decline in property values also can be expected when large amounts of land are being exchanged at increasingly higher prices with no one attempting to improve the land or to prepare it for any kind of productive use.

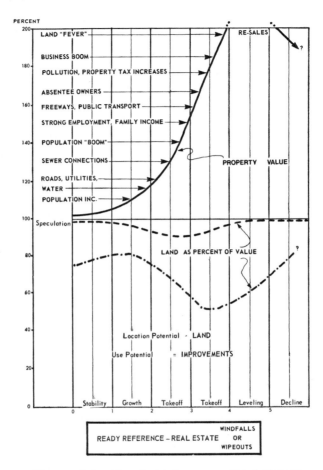

Figure 5-1 Ready Reference: Real Estate Windfalls or Wipeouts

Notice what happens to land as a percentage of total property value. As speculation increases, land tends to become a larger percentage of value. As investment value becomes paramount, improvements tend to play a large role in total property value. This happens because the land represents a location potential, but the improvements on the land represent the extent to which the location potential has been realized.

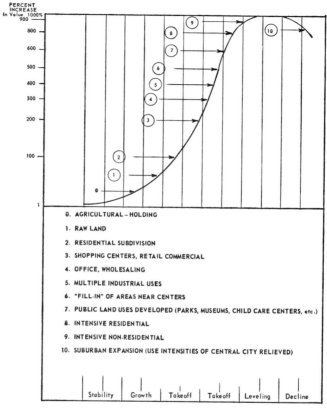

LAND USE SUCCESSION AND
"AVERAGE" PROPERTY VALUE INCREASE POTENTIALS, GROWTH AREAS

**Figure 5-2   Land Use Succession and
"Average" Property Value Increase Potentials,
Growth Areas**

Other ways of anticipating what will help increase property values are the changes in the types of land uses (Figure 5-2). Land values tend to increase as the land is used more intensively; (it produces more income per unit of measure, such as square feet). If only one home can be built on five acres in some land areas and five or more in other land areas, the price per acre probably will be lower on the less intensive use per five acre land parcel. The progression of uses is indicated in

Table 5-2, giving some clue towards what kinds of property to buy or develop as the other stages of the cycle occur.

If the two graphs were charted as one, then this type of succession can be seen:

Growth steps:	*Land use Number:*
A,B	1
C	2
D, E	3
F	4
G	5
H	6
I	7
J	8
K	9, 10

How do you use these charts in planning your home purchase? They are intended only to indicate in a general way the way in which land uses can change and thus increase the property values. You would want to plan to buy a home in an area that is just beginning to develop so that you can "ride" the curve upward to higher values. As the desirability of the area changes from home use to other more intensive types of uses, you will probably want to sell your home (at a good profit) and buy another in a newer area. Or, you may wish to invest in other kinds of real estate. However, in this book I am emphasizing the purchase of a home as a means of building a financial estate. In Chapter 6 I give particular instructions on how to evaluate a neighborhood to determine where it may be on the growth curve.

DO I WANT TO LIVE IN THIS NEIGHBORHOOD? — OR LOCATION, LOCATION, LOCATION

|||||||||||||||||||||||||||||||||||||||||||||||||||||||||||||||||||||||||||||||||||||||||||||||||||||||||||||||||||||||||||||||||||||||||||

6

PICKING A GOOD NEIGHBORHOOD

At this point, you should be fully aware of the importance of selecting a neighborhood that will help improve the investment value of the home you buy. In this chapter I offer some specific means of checking the neighborhood.

WHAT IS THE NEIGHBORHOOD LIKE?

There are four major things you will want to know about a neighborhood. Below is a brief discussion of each and then a checklist for your use in making notes about each neighborhood.

Boundaries

Land uses are sometimes controlled by locally imposed zoning regulations. These determine how large your lot and house must be, where you are to locate your house, and many other items about using the house. Ask local city hall what zoning regulations prevail. You will want to buy in a neighborhood in which residential uses are protected. Major streets and arteries are sometimes used to set the boundaries, but in any case, they determine in a general way the boundaries for particular kinds of home developments. Look around carefully and you can sometimes tell by the differences in the houses where the boundaries are found. In any case, your home will have more value if it is located more towards the center of the neighborhood. Your investment potential is even greater as a home investment if the adjacent areas also are zoned for single-family land uses.

Physical and Geographical Characteristics

You check these characteristics to determine whether the homes look reasonably alike or are generally attractive because this adds to value; climate, contours, hills, and view can add value by providing pleasant living, as well as reasonable privacy. Most importantly, you want to avoid an area that is subject to noises, odors, or other annoyances associated with heavy traffic, overflights of private or commercial planes, and business and industrial activities.

Transportation is becoming increasingly important to evaluate as gasoline becomes more expensive and difficult to obtain. Evaluate your family travel habits and then use the list to determine how and how long it will take to get to places your family considers important. Careful evaluation of public transportation potentials may mean that you can eliminate one family car or that you won't be stuck if gasoline shortages appear again.

Political and Legal Characteristics

Most of your questions about political and legal matters can be answered by local real estate brokers, mortgage-loan officers, or even the owners of the house you may want to buy.

The local city administrative office can tell you about zoning or building codes and the extent to which they are being enforced in the area you are evaluating. Deed restrictions and neighborhood or home owner associations are means that private persons use to protect home values in the area. They may restrict what you wish to do, but more likely they will help protect your home investment. In any case, ask about them; ask to see the written rules and talk to neighbors. Usually a title insurance company or an abstract and title company can provide you with a copy of any private agreements which affect your house. Ask for copies of any CC and R (covenants, codes, and restrictions.)

Table 6-1   Do You Want to Live in This Neighborhood?

		Comments and Conclusions
Boundaries		
Political	What are the zoning boundaries? What kind of zoning exists?	
Physical	Streets, hills, gullies, rivers, similar physical features divide cities into neighborhoods	
Major streets and traffic arteries		
Physical and Geographic Characteristics		
Buildings and improvements		
Average age of main structures		
Average size: sq. ft. and rooms		
Typical architectural style		
State of maintenance		
Geographic		
Climate (average temperature, average rainfall)		
Contours, hills, valleys		
Ability of soil to bear the weight of the houses		
Hazards and nuisances		
High-speed traffic arteries		
Airports, flight patterns		
Industrial activity		
Railroads		
Ravines, gullies, hills, water		

Table 6-1 Do You Want to Live in This Neighborhood? *(cont.)*

	Comments and Conclusions
Transportation (adequacy, cost, quality, types, frequency of service); ideal time to: School (15–30 min.)	
Major sources of employment (30–60 min.)	
Shopping, neighborhood type, (5–10 min.)	
Shopping, regional type, (10–30 min.)	
Recreation, what kinds, (10–60 min.)	
Church (10–30 min.)	
Major central business district (30–45 min.)	
Medical services (5–30 min.)	
Comments:	
Political and Legal Characteristics (City hall can answer many of these) Enforcement	
Building codes, control over material use of electricity, etc.	
Planning, anticipated future uses of neighborhood	
Deed restrictions, neighborhood agreements, clubs, etc.	
Police and fire protection (5–15 min.)	
Schools, number and types	
Taxes, average tax bill, assessed values, and tax rate (2-10% of house price)	
Special assessments (amount/kind)—charges for other government services (trash, sewage, street lights)	
Comments:	
Economic Relation to direction of city growth	
Average family income	
Average home value	
Average rentals	
Utilities (rate, typical monthly costs) Water	
Gas	
Electricity	
Comments:	

Economic Considerations

Since you are interested in maximizing the investment value of the home you buy, be particularly careful to check out the economic characteristics of the neighborhood. Basically, the homes should be of about the same value, and neighbors should have the financial capacities to maintain their homes. Walk around the area near the home you want to buy. Are the homes being maintained? If so, the neighbors are earning sufficient income and have a demonstrated interest in keeping their homes in shape. You can determine value by asking real estate brokers and others.

Buying a home that is a lot cheaper than one's neighbor's homes can be dangerous. There may be much unforeseen trouble in the home. Perhaps there is something wrong that cannot be corrected. Use all the help you can get to determine the value of a bargain. If the home looks as though it has been neglected and could be repaired, ask an expert to help determine whether the property can be improved and at what cost. Long-standing neglect can produce problems that can be corrected only at great cost. Do not get caught by trying to buy a "bargain."

A house that is more expensive than the other homes is not a bargain, even if it is bigger or of a higher quality. If the home is much bigger or better than the surrounding homes in the area, its price will be lower relative to what it would bring if it was located in an area of similar homes. Unless you feel that the neighborhood will slowly be improved so that more and more homes will be as large and expensive as the home you are looking at, do not try to buy it for investment purposes.

Table 6-2 is another means for checking the area. The list is not as elaborate but covers the essential items. In the questions containing many parts, a "no" for any part of it means a "no" for the question. Simply answer yes or no to each question, add up the "yes" answers and check against the score card. Actually, you may wish to change the totals so that for your tastes, fewer yesses will still indicate a good area. In any case, this is a handy means of comparing one neighborhood with another. Sharp differences in the ''yes'' answers will help estimate obviously unsatisfactory areas.

Do not base your rating on only one visit to the area. Go during the night to find out about the amount of street lighting around the home. A well-lighted area is one which discourages crime. Visit during the hours when family members are likely to be going to and from work, school, shopping, and so on. You may find the traffic too much to drive in and too noisy around your home.

Table 6-2 Rating the Neighborhood

SCORE CARD: GOOD—20 yesses; ACCEPTABLE—18 yesses; POOR—17 or less

		YES	NO
1.	Are the neighbors in the same income bracket?		
2.	Do the neighbors have roughly the same job interests?		
3.	Are the majority of the neighbors buying their own homes?		
4.	Are the majority of the houses in the area of about the same size and architecture?		
5.	Are the majority of the houses in the area reasonably well maintained?		
6.	Are the zoning regulations enforced in the area?		
7.	Are there deed restrictions in force in the area?		
8.	Has the city completed any changes in streets, freeways, similar items?		
9.	Is the area well drained during rains?		
10.	Are all of the utilities installed: ( ) paved streets ( ) city water ( ) sidewalks ( ) electricity ( ) street lights ( ) gas ( ) sewage disposal? Do I pay for any of the above?		
11.	Is public transportation reasonably priced and on regular schedule?		
12.	Is there public transportation to: ( ) shopping ( ) theatres ( ) work ( ) churches ( ) schools ( ) recreation? (One ''no'' for each item not checked.)		
13.	Is it less than 15-minutes travel time to: ( ) work ( ) churches ( ) shopping ( ) theatres ( ) schools ( ) recreation? (One ''no'' for each item not checked.)		
14.	Are the property taxes equitably assessed? Current assessed value of the lot? $_____annual per $100 of assessed value		

Table 6-2 *(cont.)*

		YES	NO
15.	Are the tax rates reasonable? Current rates? $_____ Total annual tax bill $_____		
16.	Is the area free of special assessments?		
17.	Is the area insulated from high-speed traffic?		
18.	Is the area free from airport overhead traffic and noises?		
19.	Is the area free from industrial noises, odors, and traffic?		
20.	Is the area free from dangerous ravines, gullies, and standing water?		
21.	Is the area, and properties in the area, ten years old or less on the average?		
22.	Is the city growing up around this area?		
23.	Are at least 95 per cent of the lots in the area already built on?		
24.	Is police protection available on call in less than 5 minutes?		
25.	Is fire protection available on call in less than 5 minutes?		
	TOTAL		

WHAT IS THE CONDITION OF THE LOT AND THE HOUSE?

||||||||||||||||||||||||||||||||||||||||||||||||||||||||||||||||||||||||||||||||||||||||||||||||||||||||||||||||||||||||||||

7

The varieties of homes families buy is clear evidence that tastes vary widely in terms of what is a suitable house. For this reason, checking the condition of the lot and the house can become a very personal, subjective process. I suggested that maximum investment value is achieved by purchasing a house that is rather like its neighbors. I stress that you will probably find the costs of using an expert to check the house relatively inexpensive, particularly since you wish to avoid the added costs of improving, modernizing, or renovating the house after you buy it.

There are two kinds of checklists provided in this chapter. The first type is intended only to provide reminders of things to look at, leaving up to you the decision of determining the value of that particular item. Some examples from each of the major checklists will help you understand how to use them.

Is the Lot Suitable?

You should check the dimensions to be certain you are getting all of the space you pay for. You might want to use a surveyor to check the lot lines and to place metal posts at all corners of the lot.

If you have any suspicions about the quality of the soil and subsoil, by all means call in a soil engineer or a geologist. Ask them if settling is occuring and if it will affect the house in any way.

Site utilization will help you decide how you can use the outdoor space. If you are thinking of adding a garage, a tennis court, or a swimming pool, be sure that the lot is of sufficient size and that local building codes and deed restrictions will allow you to do this. Use the yes–no checklist (Table 7-1) to help you compare lots.

Is the House Suitable?

Suitability refers primarily to your ideas of what a house should be like. Some of the questions may have to be answered by experts (Table 7-2). Do not hesitate to use them if you are at all concerned about durability, structural soundness, service systems, or equipment. The other items in the checklist can be checked by you. Decide what standards you want the house to meet and go through these items as reminders. In the last part of the chapter I provide yes–no checklists for each type of room in the house. These checklists incorporate most of these ideas in a way that permits you to evaluate the house you particularly like and any others you may be considering.

The Functional Plan

Function relates to the usefulness of the house for your family's style of living. In most items, your family will not differ too greatly from other families like yours. You can have some confidence in your judgments about functional qualities.

For example, architecture is very much a matter of taste. If the house has an instant appeal to you, architecture probably plays a large part in this evaluation. Stand back from the house and see how it fits in with its neighbors and the lot. Does it look good to you? If so, the architecture and design are probably just fine.

Opinions are divided on some items. Some families prefer a living room at the front of the house; others prefer that it be at the rear. Some want the living room to be independent of the heavily used family room; others want the living room big enough to serve as the family activity center around the clock.

Some families do not want a separate dining room, preferring it to be incorporated as a part of the living room space. Others want a large dining room physically separated from other areas in the house. Such choices are a matter of individual preference, although what you can buy may have been dictated by the fashions prevailing when the house was built.

All these suggestions relate to what you think makes a home "liveable." Use the list to remind you of what you want to check to make sure you are getting a house that is liveable for your family.

Table 7-1   What is the Condition of the Lot and the House? Is the Lot Suitable?

The lot provides the setting in which the various improvements to it, including the house, are arranged. There are many things about a lot that could prevent you from having the type of home that you want; therefore, you should be careful to check all of the items listed. In the following section you will find a summary list of the items about which you need information. You will also find a checklist which you can use to rate your lot.

Information needed for judging a lot:

1.   Legal description and street address. You will need the legal description of the lot for a number of purposes; therefore be sure you get it and be sure it is correct. The usual description will read: "Lot No. 27, Block 758 of Tract No. 384562" (or the tract may also have a name, such as Sunset Acres). If there is a dispute as to what property you own, you will be required to furnish a legal description. If

Table 7-1 *(cont.)*

the property mentioned in the legal description is not the same as the one at the street address, the property you own will be the one at the legal address. The title insurance company or the real estate broker or your lawyer can usually check this for you.

2. Dimensions and shape including a drawing showing all improvements on the lot. (A regular shape is best.)

3. Soil and subsoil. Does house show settling or are there big cracks in the foundation? Are there unusual hazards (particularly for hillside properties)—get a soil engineer report—like mud slides?

4. Drainage. Is there danger of flooding or excessive erosion?

5. Topography. How much of the site is usable, any topographical hazards because of adjacent properties? A steep cliff?

6. Immediately adjacent uses. Is there a reasonable degree of privacy and freedom from annoyance from adjacent uses?

7. Site utilization. Private and public use restrictions, yard space as related to location of walks, driveways, landscaping and other improvements should all be considered.

8. Access from the lot to public streets and public ways.

Score Card
Good: 16 yesses; Acceptable: 14 yesses; Poor : 13 or less

	YES	NO
Does the house cover 30 per cent or less of the lot?		
Is at least one-half of the lot level?		
Does the lot drain during rains?		
Does the soil support the house sufficiently well to prevent drainage into the house and to prevent the house from settling?		
Is the lot reasonably regular in shape?		
Is the soil of sufficient quality to permit growing: ( ) grass ( ) shrubs ( ) flowers ( ) a garden? Any item not checked score NO		
Is the lot easily accessible from the street?		
Is the lot oriented to provide good sunlight?		
Is the lot oriented to provide good ventilation for the house with respect to prevailing breezes?		
Is the lot protected from drainage from higher lots?		
Is the lot protected against eroding during heavy rains?		
Is the lot free from domination by higher surrounding lots?		
Is there a clear view to the street?		

Table 7-1 *(cont.)*

Is the exact size of the lot known and clearly indicated:
Front   ft. Rear   ft. Side   ft.
Side   ft.

Does the lot provide reasonable privacy from the adjoining properties.

Is there a clothes drying and storage area shielded from the house?

Is the lot landscaped?

Is the area free from strong, steady winds?

Is there provision for trash disposal?

Is there sufficient space for outdoor activities?

                                            Total

Table 7-2 Is the House Suitable?

In trying to decide whether the house is suitable for your needs you should check both the construction of the house and its use or functional potentials. The major categories of information that you will want to collect are listed below. Following are suggestions for inspecting the house and rating it before using the checklist below.

1. Durability: quality of workmanship and materials, evidences of property deterioration, degree to which property has withstood use and weather.

2. Structural soundness: kinds and condition of materials used in and evidences of failure in foundation, wall (exterior and interior), floors, ceilings, and roof.

3. Building space: room sizes and use potentials, traffic patterns, natural light and ventilation, electrical fixtures and outlets.

4. Service systems: capacities, use convenience and condition of electrical, plumbing, heating, and ventilating systems.

5. Mechanical and convenience equipment: make, capacity, and condition of heating devices, water heaters, air conditioners, stoves, refrigerators, freezers, clothes washers, clothes dryers, and similar types of equipment.

6. Architecture and appearance: evidence of poor or outdated architectural styling or neglect of the exterior appearance of the property.

7. Conformance to neighborhood standards: quality of maintenance, size and style of property compared to typical neighborhood properties.

8. Assessed value: assessed value of house and of total property compared to cost and market value.

9. Floor plan of house: room locations and size, doorways, windows, closets, electrical outlets and fixtures, and equipment locations (show dimensions or draw the plan to scale).

You should be aware of these items before using the checklist.

Table 7-2 *(cont.)*

CHECKLIST FOR FUNCTIONAL PLAN OF A HOUSE

Architecture and design

Modern or obsolete in appearance
Attached or detached
Position with respect to street, lot lines, and other structures in area
General appearance

Living room

Favored location
Proportions: ratio of three to two preferred; long, narrow rooms hard to furnish
Placement of doors, windows, registers, radiators, electrical outlets as related to circulation, ventilation, heating, lighting, and furniture placement
Fireplace: position with respect to traffic and possible furniture grouping; provision of ash dump and wood storage
Circulation: direct, requiring as little floor space as possible, convenient with respect to furniture groupings.
Position of windows and doors to assure privacy
Location of closets and stairs with respect to living room
Adequacy of floor and wall space

Dining room or area

Necessity of dining room for size house involved
Proportions: dining rooms best if square or nearly so; consider proportions in relation to furniture
Position of doors and windows, electric outlets, electric fixtures, radiators, registers as related to circulation, ventilation, heating, lighting, and furniture placement
Ease of access to kitchen
Privacy: position of doors and windows

Bedrooms

Adequacy of floor area and wall space for essential furniture
Provision for cross ventilation
Position of doors and windows with respect to privacy, furniture placement, ventilation
Position of radiators, registers, and electrical outlets in relation to heating, lighting, and furniture placement
Position of room in relation to bathroom; protection against noise from bathroom and other living areas

Kitchen

Efficiency of arrangement with respect to "work centers;" placement of

Table 7-2 *(cont.)*

equipment—L shaped or U shaped are best; sequence of work centers (for example, in order refrigerator, sink, range)

Position of windows and doors with respect to work arrangement

Provision of ventilation: exhaust fan

Provision of light for work centers

Condition of walls, floors, and ceilings; attractiveness, ease of cleaning

Work surfaces, height, convenience, quality, and ease of cleaning

Adequacy of floor and wall area for essential equipment

Bathroom

Location with respect to other rooms; provision for privacy

Fixtures: quality, placement

Adequacy of floor area

Position of windows and doors with respect to arrangement of fixtures, privacy, and ventilation

Lighting arrangements

Floors and walls: adequacy of floor and wall covering, and ease of cleaning

Safety: protection against falling, such as grab-bars and rails

Storage space: medicine closet, towel closet, clothes hamper, waste basket, and other space

Provision of shut-off valves for water: convenience of location and ease of repair

Provision of towel rack and other accessories

Heating

Halls and stairs

Safety provisions: lights, handrails, steepness or narrowness of stairs, balanced use of hall space, and position of stairs and halls with respect to other rooms

Condition of outside stairs and provisions for safety

Basement area

Size and condition: adequacy of floor area and height, and dryness

Provision for light and ventilation, window space, and location

Arrangement of equipment, adequacy of space for furniture, storage, and so on

Convenience of stairs

Possibilities of special uses: playrooms, laundry, and so on

Closets

Number and location with respect to need

At least one per bedroom

Coat closet: location and size

Linen closets

Broom and special equipment closet

Storage closets: size, location, and ease of use

Table 7-2 *(cont.)*

Dimensions of closets: not less than 22 inches deep not over 30 inches deep for clothes closet, others in accordance with use

Other storage provisions

Basement storage: dryness, convenience, lighting, and safety
Attic storage: adequacy, safety, lighting, and ease of access
Kitchen and accessory storage: food storage, seasonal equipment, tools and equipment such as cleaning utensils, paints, and so on
Fuel storage
Laundry storage
Waste: garbage, trash, and so on

Accessory buildings: garage, and so on

Condition
Adequacy for purposes
Special provisions for work shops, tool storage, and so on

WHAT IS THE CONDITION OF THE OUTSIDE OF THE HOUSE?

Score Card:
Good: 21 yesses; Acceptable: 18 yesses; Poor: 17 or less

	YES	NO
Is the earth banked around the foundation so as to permit water to drain away from the house?		
Is the foundation firm and not crumbling?		
Is the foundation free from sagging and large cracks?		
Is the paint free from blisters and curling?		
Has the house been painted in the last two years?		
Wooden walls:		
Are the boards free of curling or twisting?		
Are the boards free of cracks and knotholes?		
Are the boards firm and not in need of nailing?		
Stucco walls:		
Are the walls free of major cracks?		
Is the stucco firm and tight to the walls?		
Masonry walls:		
Is the mortar between the cracks firm?		
Is the mortar filled and in place?		
Is the exterior wood firm and free of dry rot?		
Is the exterior wall free of termite holes and channels?		
Is there caulking around the windows to keep out rain and dust?		
Is the roof five years or less of age?		

Table 7-2 *(cont.)*

	YES	NO
Is the roof free of cracks and signs of recent repairs?		
Are the downspouts in good condition to carry off the roof water away from drainage into the foundation? (Storm windows in cold climates?)		
Are there screens for the windows and doors?		
In areas of strong sunlight are there awnings or shutters to diffuse the sunlight?		
Do the chimney for the fireplace, and other chimneys, appear straight; and are all of the masonry cracks filled, especially between the bricks?		
Do the walls have insulation? The roof?		
Is the overall appearance of the exterior pleasing?		
Is there an outside light at the front door?		
Is the house oriented on the lot to obtain maximum advantage of sunlight?		
Is the house oriented to obtain maximum benefit from the prevailing breezes?		
Is there foundation shrubbery planting?		
Is the house oriented to take maximum advantage of the view?		
Are there outside faucets for lawn, flower, and garden watering?		
Is there a paved area under the clothesline? And in the outdoor storage area?		
Total		

WHAT IS THE CONDITION OF THE INSIDE OF THE HOUSE?

Living Room

Score Card:
Good: 16 yesses; Acceptable: 13 yesses; Poor: 12 or less

	YES	NO
Is the room light, with ample window space?		
Do the windows open and close tightly?		
Are the floors level?		
Are the floors in good condition and not in need of refinishing?		
Are the walls smooth and free of cracks, especially over the doors and window openings?		
Is there at least one electrical outlet on each wall?		

Table 7-2 *(cont.)*

	YES	NO
Are the walls sufficiently clear of openings to permit a variety of furniture placements?		
Do you know the exact size of the room?　　　　Length Width		
Does the living area contain at least 200 square feet? Or is there a family room of this size?		
Is the living area shielded from direct observation from the front door?		
Are the measurements of the living room at least in a ratio of three to two?		
Is there a closet near the entrance of the living room of sufficient size to hold guests' coats, and so on?		
Will persons using the room be free from the disturbance of traffic crossing the room to other parts of the house?		
Are the windows of such a size and so placed as to prevent observation into all of the room from the street?		
Is there a fireplace and is it placed so as to permit free flow of foot traffic around the room and also to encourage good furniture placement?		
Does the fireplace work properly and draw adequately?		
Is there provision for a television outlet?		
Is there a heating outlet into the room?		
Total		

Dining Room

Score Card:
Good: 11 yesses; Acceptable: 9 yesses; Poor: 8 or less

	YES	NO
Is the dining area well lighted by natural light?		
Do the windows open and close easily and properly?		
Are the floors level?		
Are the floors in good condition and not in need of refinishing?		
Are the walls smooth and free of cracks, especially over doors and window openings?		
Is there an electrical outlet on each wall?		
Is there overhead artificial illumination for the dining area?		

Table 7-2 *(cont.)*

	YES	NO
Does the dining area contain a minimum of 80 square feet? Length Width		
Is the dining area nearly square?		
Is the dining area easily accessible from the kitchen?		
Is the dining room adjacent to but reasonably private from the living room?		
Can traffic pass from the other areas in the house through the dining area with ease and without too much interference with the dining furniture?		
Can at least four persons be placed around the dining table and be served easily?		
Is the dining area accessible for outdoor living and dining?		
Is there storage space for dishes, glassware, linens?		
Total		

Bedrooms

	YES	NO
Score Card: Good: 14 yesses; Acceptable: 12 yesses; Poor: 11 or less		
Are the rooms well lighted by natural light?		
Are the rooms cross ventilated?		
Are the floors level?		
Are the floors in good condition and not in need of refinishing?		
Do the windows open and close easily and properly?		
Are the walls smooth and free of cracks, especially over doors and window openings?		
Is there an electrical outlet on each wall?		
Is there sufficiently clear wall space (at least 100 square feet) to permit placement of beds and chests?		

Do the major bedrooms have a minimum of 100 square feet?
    Length   Width   Length
    Width		

Do the smaller bedrooms have a minimum of 80 square feet?
    Length   Width   Length
    Width		

Do each of the bedroom closets provide at least 6 square feet of floor space and at least 5½ feet of clear clothes hanging space, with one shelf, rod and hooks, and a minimum depth of 22 inches?		

Table 7-2 *(cont.)*

	YES	NO
Is there a heating outlet in each room?		
Are the sleeping areas insulated from noise in other areas or outside the house?		
Are the bedrooms so located as to provide privacy for the users of these rooms?		
Are the bedrooms easily accessible to the bathrooms?		
Is there a storage closet for bedroom linens which is easily accessible to the bedrooms? Minimum closet: 14 inches across x 18 inches deep with at least five shelves 12 inches apart.		
Total		

Bathrooms

Score Card:
Good: 18 yesses; Acceptable: 15 yesses; Poor: 14 or less

	YES	NO
Is the bathroom well lighted by natural light?		
Does the bathroom have a window that can be opened?		
Are the floors level?		
Will the floor materials resist wet and moisture?		
Are the walls around the showers and wash basins of a waterproof material?		
Is there a separate shower, separate from the bathtub?		
Can each bathroom fixture be used without interfering with the use of the other fixtures?		
Are there electrical outlets near the wash basin?		
Is there enough artificial light?		
Are there safety bars near the bath and shower fixtures to prevent falling?		
Is there a medicine chest?		
Is there storage space conveniently available for linens, medicines, and similar items?		
Is there space for a clothes hamper or storage of dirty clothes?		
Are there at least two towel racks?		
Are the bathroom noises insulated from other parts of the house?		
Is there a minimum of one complete bathroom? (At least 60 square feet)		
Is there at least one additional one-half bath (stool and wash basin) for each two bedrooms in excess of two bedrooms?		

Table 7-2 *(cont.)*

	YES	NO

Are the floor and wall materials of a kind which can be cleaned easily and frequently?

Are the fixtures of at least average quality and free of defects such as rust spots and metal peeling?

Do all bathroom fixtures work easily?

Do all the drains work rapidly and efficiently?

Do you know the exact size of each bathroom?   Length
        Width   Length   Width

Is there a safe heat outlet or other means of heating the bathrooms?

Total

Kitchen

Score Card:
Good: 24 yesses; Acceptable: 20 yesses; Poor: 19 or less

	YES	NO

Is the kitchen well lighted by natural light?

Can the kitchen be ventilated by means of outside windows?

Is there a good natural light over the work areas?

Are the floor materials resistant to use and moisture and easily cleaned?

Are the floors level?

Is the kitchen arranged to permit efficiency in work, that is, minimum steps from refrigerator to stove, and to the sink?

Is there an exhaust fan to carry off kitchen odors, smoke, and so on?

Are there artificial lights or illumination over all work areas?

Are the work surfaces of proper height to prevent stooping or bending while being used?

Can work surfaces be cleaned easily?

Are the electrical outlets easily available to each work area?

Is there a storage closet for brooms, mops, and similar kinds of cleaning equipment and materials?

Is there a minimum of 6 feet of continuous unobstructed work space on the counter?

Is there a minimum of 18 feet of continuous storage shelf space at least 11 inches deep and equipped with doors which close tightly? (Shelves should not be over 6 feet 6 inches from the floor.)

74

Table 7-2 *(cont.)*

	YES	NO
Is there a convenient electrical outlet and space for an electric refrigerator?		
Is there space for a gas stove or three-pronged electrical outlet for an electric stove?		
Is there under-the-counter storage space, with doors?		
Is there a garbage disposal unit or sanitary, easily available, garbage disposal facility?		
Are there drawers for storage under the counter working areas?		
Is there eating space in the kitchen?		
Is there a utility room or space easily available to the kitchen?		
Are there fixtures already available for the installation of an automatic clothes washer or dryer?		
Is there an outside entrance available to the kitchen?		
Can traffic move easily through the kitchen without interfering with the work areas in the kitchen?		
Is the kitchen sink a two-compartment sink, or of a large size?		
Do all of the fixtures work properly?		
Do the drains work rapidly and efficiently?		
Are the fixtures ten years or less in age?		
Are the fixtures free of rust and the metal free of peeling?		
Is there an automatic dishwasher?		
Is there an electrical outlet located so that an electric clock can be placed on the kitchen wall?		
Total		

Plumbing

Score Card:
Good: 7 yesses; Acceptable: 6 yesses; Poor: 5 or less

	YES	NO
Are the plumbing fixtures ten years of age or less?		
Does each fixture have a cutoff which can be reached easily?		
Do the pipes ring clear when tapped?		
Is there an automatic water heater of at least 30 gallons capacity (with recovery rate sufficient to keep water hot under continuous use)?		
Can showers, dishwasher, and clothes washer all use hot water at the same time without loss of volume?		

Table 7-2 *(cont.)*

	YES	NO
Is the water supplied from a city system?		
Is the sewage disposal system connected with a public system? And are there outside cleanout fixtures?		
Are there exterior water outlets front and rear?		
Have you tested each fixture and do you know that each works?		
Is the water system equipped with a water softening system?		
Will the flow of water continue undiminished when all faucets are turned on?		
Total		

Electrical System

Score Card:
Good: 7 yesses; Acceptable: 6 yesses; Poor: 5 or less

	YES	NO
Are the fixtures in the house ten years of age or less?		
Do the fixtures harmonize with the decor?		
Is there a wall switch in each room by means of which the lights in the room may be regulated?		
Is the wiring protected by cable, pipe, or similar type of covering?		
Is the electrical system protected by an automatic cutoff system, with a switch breaker, rather than by means of fuses?		
Is the system able to carry all of the electrical equipment which you expect to use?		
Is there an exterior fixture which illuminates the rear yard?		
Is there an exterior fixture which permits illumination of the front door or area leading from the street to the front door?		
Is there a working doorbell system?		
Is there an internal music/radio/communication system?		
Total		

Heating

Score Card:
Good: 5 yesses; Acceptable: 4 yesses; Poor: 3 or less

	YES	NO
Is the heating a central system which is properly vented?		
Is the system a thermostat-controlled forced-air system or controlled electrical heat?		

Table 7-2 *(cont.)*

	YES	NO
If the system is oil or butane, is the storage capacity sufficient for one full season of normal heating?		
Are there heating outlets in each of the rooms in the house?		
Is there modern, thermostat-controlled air conditioning?		
If the system is gas, are the fixtures and furnace less than five years old?		
Air conditioning?		
Total		

IS THERE A GARAGE OR CARPORT AND IS IT SUITABLE?

Score Card:
Good: 12 yesses; Acceptable: 10 yesses; Poor: 9 or less

	YES	NO
What are the exact measurements of the garage? Length Width (at least 8' x 15' clear area for each car)		
Will the garage hold two cars and permit you to get in and out of the cars while they are in the garage?		
Is there sufficient rough storage space for lawn equipment, trunks, and similar items when your car is in the garage?		
Can the garage doors be opened easily by one person?		
Is there another entrance to the garage besides that through which the cars enter?		
Is there an overhead electrical fixture to light the interior of the garage with a switch available near the entrance?		
Is the approach to the garage lighted?		
Can a car be driven from the street into the garage easily?		
Is there space to turn the car around next to the garage so that the car need not be backed into the street?		
Is the garage architecture complementary to the house architecture?		
Do the garage walls seem strong and free of holes, cracks, and so on?		
Has the garage been painted and maintained as well as the house?		
Is the garage weather and rain proof?		
Can the garage be locked securely?		
Is the driveway to the garage paved?		
Total		

Total Score for the Property

Total Yesses

	GOOD	ACCEPTABLE	POOR
Buy or rent..................................			
Neighborhood			
The lot.......................................			
Outside of the house			
Inside of the house			
Living room			
Dining room			
Bedrooms			
Bathrooms...............................			
Kitchen			
Plumbing			
Electrical			
Heating			
Garage			

Total Yesses for Property:
Rating of the Property:

Good	183–220	Yesses
Acceptable	156–182	Yesses
Poor	0–155	Yesses

CAN YOU ESTIMATE THE MARKET VALUE OF YOUR HOME?

||||||||||||||||||||||||||||||||||||||||||||||||||||||||||||||||||||||||||||||||||||||||||||||||||||||||||||||||||||||||||||||||||||

8

Estimating the market value of a home you are planning to purchase, or one that you are planning to sell, is a job for experts; but there are some things you can do. We have already mentioned that you might want to use an appraiser. An inexpensive kind of appraisal report that you can ask for is shown in Table 8-1. This is a simple appraiser checklist. You notice there are many items on it that we have discussed. The property to be appraised is at 15921 A Avenue. I have omitted the value that the appraiser placed on the property so that you can determine what value you might estimate based on the information furnished by the appraiser.

VALUE AND COST

There are times when you may have the choice of buying an existing home or building a new one. Your problem is to decide which

Table 8-1 A Professional Appraiser's Evaluation Report For a Home at 15921 A Avenue

Property	Subject Property	Comparable No. 1	Comparable No. 2	Comparable No. 3
ADDRESS	15921 Alcima Ave Pacific Palisades	15912 Alcima Avenue Pacific Palisades	1055 Palisair Place Pacific Palisades	1150 Lachman Lane Pacific Palisades
MAP CODE	40-C-3	40-C-3	40-C-3	40-B-3
PROXIMITY TO SUBJECT		4421-13-(3)-A.P.	4421-8-(3) A.P.	4421-41-(30) A.P.
DESCRIPTION: TYPE CONSTRUCTION	Conventional stucco & wood sid.	Redwood siding (Rustic)	Conventional stucco	Conventional stucco
NUMBER OF STORIES	2	1	1 1/2	1
ROOM COUNT SIZE	7 1/2 DA-RR-1 3/4- 3,444 sf 3/4-1/2	7-3-Den-DR-3 2,426 sq. ft.	8-4-FR-2 1/2 2,637 sq. ft.	9-4-DR-Den-FR-3 2,850 sq. ft.
YEAR BUILT	1957	1951	1958	1964
CONDITION	Good	Good	Good	Good
QUALITY OF CONSTRUCTION	Good	Good	Good	Good
ROOF	Shake	Shake	Shake	Tar & Gravel
AIRCONDITIONING	None	None	None	None
HEATING	F.A. Central	F.A. Central	F.A. Central	F.A. Central
FIREPLACE	2	1	2	1
BUILT-INS	R/O, DW	R/O, DW	R/O, DW	R/O, DW
POOL	None	None	None	None
OTHER MAJOR IMPROVEMENTS	Large balcony area	Patio	Patio	Patio
LANDSCAPING	Good	Good	Good	Good
UTILITY	Good	Good	Good	Good
OFF ST. PARKING (NUMBER OF CARS)	2 Carport	2 Car Garage	2 car Garage	2 car Garage
GENERAL PROPERTY APPEAL	Good	Good Rustic	Good	Good
NEIGHBORHOOD	Good	Good	Good	Good
LOT SIZE	12,000 sq. ft. pad	18,295 sq. ft.	±18,000 sq. ft.	±10,000 sq. ft. pad
ZONING	±19,000 sf total	Nearly all level	±8,000 sq. ft. pad	
VIEW	Partially obstructed by trees	Very slight view	Good unobstructed view to southwest	Excellent ocean and city view.
COMMENTS	Site is set-back from street and reached by long driveway.	Below street grade perimeter location (site) Smaller improve. Better quality improve. Larger site. (level)	Cul-de-sac location. (site) Smaller, similar quality improvements. Superior view. Smaller pad.	Perimeter location (site) Smaller, similar quality improvements. Superior view. Similar size pad.
PRICE	$	$95,000	$72,500	$74,500
TERMS		Conventional 42% down	Conventional 20% down	Conventional 20% down.
DATE DATA SOURCE		12/71 SREA	8/71 SREA	8/71 SREA
TOTAL ADJUSTMENT		− $ +	− $ +	− $ +
COMPARISON TO SUBJECT				
INDICATED VALUE OF SUBJECT		$	$	$
PRICE PER SQ. FT. (WHEN APPLICABLE)	$	$39.15	$27.49	$26.14

80

Table 8-1 *(cont.)*

Comparable No. 4	Comparable No. 5	Comparable No. 6	Comparable No. 7
1174 Las Pulgas Place	1209 Turquesa Lane	1049 Haven Drive	1001 Enchanted Way
40-C-3	40-B-3	40-B-3	40-B-3
4421-35-(2) A.P.	4421-42-(23)	4419-38-(16) A.P.	1419-3-(18)
Conventional Stucco & wood siding	Conventional Siding &	Conventional Stucco	Conventional Stucco
Two	One	One	One
8-4-DR-FR-3	8-4-DR-FR-3	8-4-DR-3 1/2	8-4-FR-2 1/2
2,505 sq. ft.	2,665 sq. ft.	2,744 sq. ft.	2,568 sq. ft.
1960	1967	1960	1964
Good	Good	Good	Good
Good	Good	Good	Good
Shake	Tar & Gravel	Tar & Gravel	Tar & Grav
None	None	None	None
F.A. Central	F.A. Central	F.A. Central	F.A. Cen
2	1	1	
R/O, DW	R/O, DW	R/O, DW	R/O, DW
None	None	None	None
Patio	Patio	Patio	Patio
Good	Good	Good	Good
Good	Good	Good	Good
2 Car Garage	2 Car Garage	3 Car Garage	2 Car Garage
Good	Good	Good	Good
Good	Good	Good	Good
13,775 sq. ft. ±	17,000 sq. ft. ±	10,000 sq. ft. ±	20,000 sq. ft. ±
Excellent canyon & city & ocean view.	Excellent view of ocean & beach	Excellent front & rear views of city & ocean.	Excellent view of ocean & beach.
Cul-de-sac location (site) Superview view. Smaller, similar quality improvements. Similar size site.	Perimeter location (size) Smaller, superior quality improvements. Superior view, larger site.	Perimeter location. (site Smaller, superior quality improvements. Superior view. Similar size lot.	Perimeter lot location. Smaller, similar quality improvements. Superior view. Larger overall site.
$73,000	$82,500	$84,000	$85,000
Conventional 20% down	Conventional 20% down	Conventional 20% down	Conventional 20% down
6/71	2/72	1/72	1/72
SREA	SREA	SREA	SREA
+ $	+ $	+ $	+ $
$	$	$	$
$29.14	$20.96	$30.61	$33.10

81

might be the wiser investment. Obviously, an existing home will be suffering from some neglect and needed repairs, and it is old; however, it may have more value to you than a new home.

The most difficult problem of estimating the cost to build a new home is the rate at which prices for labor and materials change and the difference in the capabilities of builders. Chapter 10 discusses how to select a builder so we are not concerned with that problem. The question we are concerned with is how to estimate a value for a home to be built and before you have selected a builder.

Table 8-2 is a guide that you might use in asking various builders to estimate what they would charge you to build a home. To assist in the process you will have to have floor plans for a new home or for the one in which you are interested.

Table 8-2   Estimating the Cost to Build a New Home

Cost new for major elements

Square feet in the main structure × average price to build per
    square foot (Use the external dimensions of the main struc-
    ture.)   _____

Square feet in garage × cost to build a garage per square foot
    (Usually this is a lower price than for the house.)   _____

Cost of walks, drives, walls, patios   _____

Cost of landscaping   _____

Subtotal of costs

Cost of the lot   _____

Costs of preparing the lot for building, including digging
    trenches for foundations   _____

Costs of installing water, sewer, electrical lines   _____

Total of all costs

    If you are using an existing home as a model and would like to know what its value might be as a comparison to a new house, then subtract the following items from the above total costs:

Overcoming obvious defects which should be cured (painting,
    new plumbing, etc.)   _____

Table 8-2 *(cont.)*

Subtract about 1 per cent of total estimate value new, using
the cost method for each year the house has been built. _____

Cost estimate after deducting costs to restore the home to a
new condition _____

In making a cost estimate we assume that, if everything else is not changed and you can wait while a new house is being built, you would not pay more for an existing house than what you would pay for a new house of closely equal characteristics.

We must stress that you will probably receive widely varying estimates of the costs of building. Perhaps your best approach under such conditions is to average the estimates and assume that is a reasonably close approximation of what you may pay.

RENTAL VALUE AND MARKET VALUE

A surprising percentage of single-family homes are rented. Since you are interested in investment value, you may be interested in determining how the income-earning potential of the home could be translated into a market-value estimate. We must warn you that very few single-family homes make good rental investments unless you can do almost all of the repairs and maintenance yourself.

However, if you wish to translate the rental potential, here is how:

1. Determine the average annual gross collected rent potentials for the home you are inspecting:
    Monthly rent $300 × 12 = $3,600 gross rental potential.
2. Visit local real estate offices and ask them for information on the gross annual rents and values for any single-family homes they are renting. Use the information in this way:

Property	Annual rent	Estimated market value	Value/rent
A	$4,200	$33,000	7.9
B	3,800	31,000	8.0
C	4,600	37,000	8.1
·D	3,600	28,000	7.9
E	3,500	28,000	8.0

3. Average value to rent ratio: 7.98 or 8.
4. Rental potential of the property you wish to buy: $3,600 × 8 = $28,800 or an estimated market value of $29,000.
5. Another method would be for you to determine what interest rate you wish to earn on the income produced by the home you wish to buy. Assume that you wish to earn the equivalent of a good mortgage rate of 9.5 per cent. You estimate the value as follows: $3,600 (gross rent) divided by .095 (9.5 per cent) = $37,894.74, or $38,000 estimated market value.

CORRELATING YOUR ESTIMATES

Suppose that you end up with a market value estimate of $36,000 as a result of comparing property sales prices, $40,000 estimate using a cost method, and $38,000 using a rental-income estimate. You might average the three amounts ($36,000 + 40,000 + 38,000 divided by 3) and use an estimate of $38,000. However, you might also say that, since you can buy a home for $36,000, you will use that estimate. In any case, you know that you should not pay more than within the range of $36,000 to $40,000.

LOCATING THE INFORMATION YOU NEED TO BE AN INFORMED INVESTOR

||||||||||||||||||||||||||||||||||||||||||||||||||||||||||||||||||||||||||||||||||||||||||||||||||||||||||||||||||||||||||||||||||||||

9

If by now you are thinking about becoming a serious participant in real estate investment markets, you will need all kinds of information from that relating to national real estate market trends to that relating to your local markets. You will find that your local newspapers report regularly on real estate market trends so that you can maintain a clipping file of these items. You will also find the classified advertising a good source of information on changes in housing prices. However, there are other sources of information.

NATIONAL TRENDS

Once you have contacted some of the sources we recommend, you will find it easy to locate many I have not mentioned. You have to look at several sources before you find those that you can use. I suggest only the more obvious and less costly sources. As a matter of fact, you may find that you can build yourself a valuable market information file entirely from free sources:

1. *National trends:* GNP, money market changes, construction housing starts, sources, and uses of funds (including mortgage funds):

Construction Review (monthly)	($11.50 annual,
Supt. of Documents	$1.00 per copy)
U.S. Government Printing Office	
Washington, D.C. 20402	

Credit and Capital Markets 1974	(free)
Bankers Trust Company	
P.O. Box 318	
Church Street Station	
New York, New York 10015	

Economic Report of the President	(annual, $1.50)
Supt. of Documents	
U.S. Government Printing Office	
Washington, D.C. 20402	

Federal Reserve Bulletin	(monthly, annual
Division of Administrative Services	subscription
Board of Governors of the Federal Reserve System	$6.00,
Washington, D.C. 20551	$.60 per copy)

2. *National Trends:* latest reports on housing and market research sponsored by the Department of Housing and Urban Development:

HUD Research	(monthly, free)
U.S. Dept. of Housing and Urban Development	
Office of Policy Development and Research	
Washington, D.C. 20410	

3. *National trends:* national authorities write articles on matters relating to mortgage and real estate markets:

MGIC Newsletter	(monthly, free)
MGIC Plaza	
Milwaukee, Wisconsin 53201	

4. *National trends:* economists analyze national economic trends of all types. All are readable, easy to understand and authoritative. All will help you follow real estate construction and market trends:

Business in Brief   (bimonthly, free)
The Chase Manhattan Bank
New York, New York   10015

Business Bulletin   (monthly, free)
The Cleveland Trust Company
Cleveland, Ohio 44101

Economic Report   (monthly, except
Manufacturers Hanover Trust   during summer,
350 Park Avenue   free)
New York, New York 10022

Review   (monthly, free)
Federal Reserve Bank of St. Louis
P.O. Box 442
St. Louis Missouri   63166

(This letter frequently presents very easily understood analyses of economic trends and aspects of newer economic theories)

Savings and Loan Fact Book   (annual, free)
U.S. Savings and Loan League
111 East Wacker Drive
Chicago, Illinois   60601

U.S. Financial Data (weekly, free)
Federal Reserve Bank of St. Louis
P.O. Box 442
St. Louis, Missouri   63166

(This helps keep track of weekly changes in interest rates and other changes in money markets which will affect mortgage market volume and rates)

Real Estate Report   (quarterly,
Real Estate Research Corporation   (single copies
72 West Adams Street   free on
Chicago, Illinois   60603   request)

5. *Miscellaneous information*

For the latest tax laws affecting real estate:

Your Federal Income Tax, 1976 (or current year) edition ($1.25)
Local Internal Revenue Service office
   or Supt. of Documents
U.S. Government Printing Office
Washington, D.C.   20402

Tax Guide for Small Business   ($1.25)
Local Internal Revenue Service office
   or Supt. of Documents
U.S. Government Printing Office
Washington, D.C.   20402

FHA Techniques of Housing Market Analysis   ($42.50)
Supt. of Documents
U.S. Government Printing Office
Washington, D.C.   20402

6. *National periodicals useful to real estate investors:*

Sales Management Magazine	(monthly)
Survey of Current Business U.S. Dept. of Commerce Washington, D.C.	(monthly)
Economic Indicators U.S. Dept. of Commerce Washington, D.C.	(monthly)
Construction U.S. Dept. of Labor	(monthly)
Business Week	(weekly)
Wall Street Journal	(daily)
Monthly Review Federal Reserve Bank of San Francisco P.O. Box 7702 San Francisco, California 94120	(free)
Focus on various counties and regions Bank of America 660 So. Spring Los Angeles, California	(published irregularly)

Population Estimates of California	(periodically,
Cities and Counties	free)
Populations Research Unit	
1025 P Street	
Sacramento, California	

California Forecasts	(annual,
Ray Jallow	free)
Research and Planning Division	
United California Bank	
P.O. Box 3666	
Los Angeles, California 90051	

California, state and county, basic data needed to follow real estate market changes by counties and related business trend analyses.

Monthly Summary of Business Conditions   (monthly, free)
Research Department
Security Pacific National Bank
Three editions:

Southern California
P.O. Box 2097, Terminal Annex
Los Angeles, California   90051

Central Valley of California
P.O. Box 1691
Fresno, California   93717

Northern Coastal Counties of California
P.O. Box 76361
San Francisco, California   94120

1970 Census of Population and Housing
(Population and housing characteristics of cities
   by census tracts)
U.S. Department of Commerce
Bureau of the Census

Fortune	(monthly)
House and Home	(monthly)
Architectural Forum	(monthly)

Census volumes on housing and population
U.S. Bureau of the Census
Washington, D.C.

Housing Statistics   (monthly)
Housing and Home Finance Agency
Washington, D.C.

REGIONAL INFORMATION

There are many relatively inexpensive sources of information about business and real estate trends in your economic region. One of the regions which continues to attract real estate investors is California. A listing of information available for that state is presented below with the thought that if you will notice the sources of the information, you can find comparable sources in your area. These regional reports on both business and real estate market trends help you follow supply and demand changes in real estate markets and relate them to economic changes:

Economic Report of the Governor   (annual)
Office of the Governor
Sacramento, California

Western Business Forecast   (quarterly, free)
   (A survey of businessmen's opinions)
The Prudential Insurance Company
Western Home Office
5757 Wilshire Boulevard
Los Angeles, California   90036

Business Review   (monthly, free)
Wells Fargo Bank
Economics Department
P.O. Box 44000
San Francisco, California   94144

These are for sale (citations for particular volumes available from any state college or university library):

Supt. of Documents
U.S. Govt. Printing Office
Washington, D.C.   20402 or any
Department of Commerce Field Office

(In Los Angeles, the Federal Office Building)
Various prices: Los Angeles/Long Beach, Parts 1 and 2 = $8.00)

When in any large city you should ask about and visit a U.S. government book store where you will find displays of many kinds of government publications which will be of interest to you.

California Savings and Housing Data Book   (annual)
California Savings and Loan League
P.O. Box R
Pasadena, California

Community Guides   (irregular)
Various California Counties and Cities
Economic Research Division
Security-First National Bank
P.O. Box 2097, Terminal Annex
Los Angeles, California   90051

CITY AND NEIGHBORHOOD INFORMATION

If you wish to limit your search for information to your city and neighborhood, there are still many sources of information. Titles for some of the offices may vary, but always indicate what kinds of information you want before you decide no one can help you.

Location Analysis:

1. Survey of business conditions, real estate activity in the area	Research departments of banks
2. Business conditions and real estate markets	Banks federal reserve bank, land title companies
3. Planning reports	Planning commissions
4. Population, housing and employment	U.S. Bureau of the Census, state department of finance, state department of employment, state chamber of commerce
5. Deeds recorded, building permits	County recorder, department of building and safety

6. Locational analyses guides	Urban Land Institute, Washington, D.C.; research departments of financial institutions; chambers of commerce; large businesses
7. Population, markets, family income	Research departments of local newspapers

Site Analysis:

1. Field surveys	Own resources or consulting groups
2. Tax assessments and amounts	Tax assessor
3. Building codes	Department of building and safety
4. Zoning, planning, land uses	Planning commissions
5. Traffic and traffic patterns	Department of highways or streets; automotive clubs
6. Land-use maps	Planning commissions; map companies; Sanborn maps
7. Sales, sale prices, terms	Land title insurance companies; ownership map and book service companies
8. Census maps and reports, block books	U.S. Bureau of the Census
9. Vacancy surveys, population	Local utility companies; property owner organizations; school boards; community service organizations engaged in soliciting and welfare work; licensing agencies

Improvement Analysis:

1. Market prices and terms	Multiple listing boards; local real estate boards; title insurance companies; escrow companies; local real estate brokers; map book services

2. Soil and subsoil	Soil engineers
3. Taxes and assessments	Tax assessor
4. Utilities	Water and power, phone companies
5. Construction costs	Local builders; real estate brokers; valuation companies (Marshall and Stevens, Boeckh's, Wenzlick)
6. Field surveys	Own resources or consulting firms
7. Planning and building code regulations	Municipal offices

A SAFARI
THROUGH THE LEGAL
JUNGLE

||||||||||||||||||||||||||||||||||||||||||||||||||||||||||||||||||||||||||||||||||||||||||||||||||||||||||

10

Many home buyers and sellers come out of the sales process feeling thoroughly confused about all of the legal documents they were asked to sign, primarily because they were asked to do so without an explanation of what they were doing. In other words, they had been winding their way through the legal jungle with a very inept guide. In this chapter we hope to make the safari more understandable. A summary of the process explained in this chapter is summarized in Table 10-1. Use it to keep your bearings as you move through the legal jungle.

Normally you think of real estate as land and buildings and all kinds of other physical improvements.[1] As an investor, these are less

[1]The materials in this chapter have been taken from Frederick E. Case, *Real Estate* (Boston: Alln and Bacon, Inc., 1962), Chapters 12, 13, 15.

important than what you can do to use them to produce the kinds of investment returns you want. In other words, real estate must be seen as a bundle of rights that you will use in different ways to maximize your investment returns. In the next few pages you will be led through the steps of acquiring and using these bundles of rights by identifying briefly the major legal instruments you will use.

I am not suggesting that you practice law or that you must understand fully all aspects of these legal instruments. All that I want you to learn is their names and something about what they can do for you so that you can work with lawyers, real estate agents, title insurance companies, and other experts who will prepare (or execute) these instruments for you.

Okay. Here we go. (But first look at Table 10-1).

You want to sell your real estate, so you find a real estate agent to draw up and sign a:

Table 10-1 The Process of Buying and Selling a House

What the Buyer Does	What the Seller Does	Documents Involved
	Agrees to sell house through a broker	Real estate broker (salesperson) uses a *listing agreement* which gives price and terms of sale. Buyer signs
Buyer agrees to buy the house and makes a down payment		a *deposit receipt* indicating price and terms offer.
	Seller agrees to sell	Seller signs offer made by buyer on *deposit receipt and/or sales agreement*
Agrees to terms and signs to buy and costs to be paid	Agrees to terms and costs of transfer that will be paid	Escrow statement (Cal.) or *closing agreement* (prepared by lawyers in other areas)
Finances the portion of the sales price not included in down payment	Pays mortgage owed or transfers obligations to the buyer	*Trust deed of mortgage*, which gives terms of repayment for money borrowed for purchase
	Provides assurance that buyer has "good" title and use rights	*Title insurance* (title insurance company), *abstract and opinion* (from an attorney)
	Gives buyer proof that buyer "owns" the house	*Warranty or grant deed* (depends upon location); gives "use" or other rights which buyer owns

Table 10-1 *(cont.)*

What the Buyer Pays	*What the Seller Pays*	*Documents Involved*
Part of the costs of preparing and recording publicly the legal documents, lawyer, and legal costs Property insurance	Portion of the cost of transfer not paid by buyer	*Closing statement or escrow statement.* The amount each pays depends upon what they agree to and the customs in the area where they live. Protection against fire, theft, injury, property damage.
	Termite or property condition report; Commission to real estate broker; prepayment penalties on loan; Proof that title is "clear"	*Termite or wood rot report* (not included in many states); *listing agreement* Seller's *mortgage or trust deed; title insurance or abstract; and opinion;*
Prepaid insurance and property taxes; impounds (initial amounts to be paid monthly for property insurance, taxes)		*seller's property insurance and property tax receipts sales agreement or closing statement*
	Repairs or improvement Title transfer costs	*closing statement* (escrow) *closing statement* (escrow) *credit report*
Proof of sufficient credit to pay for mortgage		

LISTING AGREEMENT

In this contract, the property owners indicate the conditions under which they agree to sell, and the amount paid the agent for completing the sale. The agent then indicates what services will be rendered. Among the more important provisions are: (1) description of real and personal property which is being offered for sale; (2) down payment and method of financing the remaining part of the purchase price; (3) listing of costs which seller will assume, particularly those relating to clearing title and closing the sale; (4) the rights that the listing broker may exercise as an agent of the seller (discussed in detail in Chapter 11); (5) the period during which the contract is in force (usually not less than 60 nor more than 120 days); and (6) the amount of commission to be paid the listing broker if a ready, willing and able buyer is secured.

This is not so much an offer to sell as a statement of intentions, since the buyer makes the offer to buy and the seller then decides whether to accept the terms. As we shall see below, the listing brokers really performed their duty in presenting a buyer who is ready to buy and able to buy on the terms as set forth by the seller. Brokers also performed their duty if the seller accepts with some modification of the original terms.

It is important to remember that this contract makes the salesperson an agent of the sellers, and, as such, responsible for guarding the best interest of the seller.

Next you find a buyer who offers you a:

DEPOSIT RECEIPT AND/OR SALES AGREEMENT

In a typical real estate transaction the buyer will usually submit his offer to buy, his terms and a nominal cash amount to indicate his good faith. Sometimes when only a deposit check is offered, some confusion may arise if the terms are not included; therefore a deposit should not be offered unless accompanied by a statement of terms which reflect the buyer's intention. Real estate brokers usually have printed forms which are prepared in duplicate, with both copies signed by the buyer and, when the offer is accepted, signed by the seller. Some important elements besides those found in any contract are:

1. Amount of the deposit and the form in which tendered;
2. Terms of the purchase and other conditions, including adequate description of the property;
3. Date by which performance is to be completed by buyers and sellers;
4. Broker's commission and method of payment;
5. Signatures—in the case of married persons both signatures are usually required, although there is some question as to whether this is always necessary in the case of the buyers.

Most of the legal papers you will sign when buying and selling real estate are a form of "contract." Below are some basic points about contracts which you should remember.

CONTRACTS

Contract law is exceedingly complex and cannot be covered thoroughly in a few pages; however, there are certain elements which should be understood. Contracts are the means by which buyers and sellers set forth the terms on which they agree to do business. In each transaction the basic elements of a contract are modified or supplemented to suit the needs of the parties. A lawyer with economic training is a most valuable adjunct at this point, since he can give legal form to economic objectives.

Basic Elements

Although a written contract is not required in all states in the sale or exchange of property, it should as a matter of good practice be used by all real estate executives. The bargaining which often accompanies real estate transactions may leave some misunderstanding in the minds of the parties, which can be cleared up only by having all conditions put in writing. Furthermore any contract involving the sale of land must be in writing—and in cases of conflict between the written and oral statements, the written agreement prevails.

A contract need not be in a particular form, but there are certain minimum elements which must be present if the contract is to be legal.

Offer and acceptance.   In order for a contract to be created there must be an agreement between two or more parties to agree to do, or refrain from doing, some act. In the case of real estate the buyer agrees to purchase at a stated price and terms, and the seller agrees to deliver rights, as listed, for a described parcel of real estate.

Competent parties.   The parties to the contract must be legally competent to perform. That is, they must understand what they are doing and have legal power to do it. For example, questions of competency might be raised if the contracting parties were minors, insane, or incapacitated because of alcohol or drugs. Questions of competency might also be raised about the rights and privileges of persons with power of attorney, agents, executors and trustees, and officers of corporations. Usually these latter questions can be resolved with the submission of appropriate documents evidencing their powers to contract.

Legality of object.   The purposes of the contract must not contemplate violation of law or public policy—as, for instance, sale of a property for purposes prohibited by law.

Consideration.   Each party must obligate himself in some way. For example, a buyer agrees to pay money and the seller agrees to transfer his interests in land. Normally the amount of the consideration would not be involved except in obvious cases of injustice.

Writing.   A contract for land, as we have seen, must be in writing, all of the terms must be in the contract, and terms should be explicit so that there can be no misunderstanding. Sometimes when a buyer and seller are negotiating, oral promises may be exchanged, but unless these are put into writing they have no legal impact in the contract. Furthermore, if there is a question about written terms, any oral agreements which resulted in the terms but which are at variance with them are not enforceable.

Signatures.   Normally the buyers and sellers will sign, but there may be circumstances under which their representatives will be signing—for example, trustees acting for minors or legal incompetents, officers of corporations, attorneys or agents with power of attorney, or executors handling estates. In each case it is important to determine that these persons have the power to act on behalf of others. These powers are always evidenced by written instruments which should be studied or reviewed to determine the rights of the agents.

Exact copies of the contract (one to be retained by each party) are made and signed by the parties, by signature when they can write, or by an identifying mark which is witnessed when they cannot write. The signatures on the contract need not be witnessed, but witnessing may help in case of dispute over the contract. Once seals were used in place of signatures; later they were used to indicate the authenticity of the contract, but today seals have no significance for the validity of the contract although they may extend the legal obligations of the parties.

Mistakes, Fraud, Misrepresentations

Occasions may arise when there may not be the "meeting of minds" which is contemplated in the law with the signing of a contract. For example, both parties may have misunderstood terms vital to the completion of the contract, such as price, down payment or similar matters. When the mistake is mutual the contract is nto valid.

More serious problems are involved when one or both parties have deliberately practiced deceit. As in the case of mistake, if the deceit involves a material matter the contract will have no legal impact but, in addition, the injured party may have legal recourse to repair the injury. Fraud may occur when a seller indicates facts about his property which are not true, or the buyer represents facts about himself or his capacity to purchase which are not true. Misrepresentation may occur with respect to the identity or location of property, the personal property to be included in a sale, tax bills, utility costs and such matters. Sometimes misrepresentation may involve a matter of opinion which is confused with a matter of fact. For example, it would be misrepresentation for the seller to say that taxes were $150 a year when they were actually $250—and this could be the basis of legal action; however, the seller might say instead that he thought the taxes were low and there would be no misrepresentation, since this is a statement of opinion. Acceptance of an opinion about a material matter which later proves to be incorrect would normally not be an occasion for legal action if the opinion could have been verified by reasonable search. The matter of taxes, for example, can be verified from the public records.

"Caveat Emptor"

At one time buyers of property bought under the rule of "caveat emptor," which meant basically that they were responsible for ascertaining all facts relating to a property; and after they bought it, if they discovered other things about the property which injured its value to them, they could not recover from the seller but had to accept the injuries. This requirement is now being slowly modified, so that sellers are now expected to disclose to buyers material facts which might limit intended uses or the value of the property, particularly when such shortcomings could not be discovered by a typical buyer.

Buyers also have the responsibility for truthfulness, and lack of fraud or misrepresentation. When either party has suffered from fraud or misrepresentation and wishes to cancel the contract, he must return what he has already received. If either party knows of fraud or misrepresentation and goes ahead with the contract, he cannot later cancel because he has been injured.

Nonperformance

If the seller refuses to perform or fails to perform as he is required to do, the buyer has a number of options:

1. He may agree to termination of the contract and ask for a return of his deposit.
2. He may ask that the seller be required to perform as required by the contract.
3. He may sue for damages. Usually this is difficult to do unless the buyer has clear evidence that he did suffer damages. For example, he may have incurred extra expenses in having to secure a substitute property.

If the buyer fails to perform the seller may require any of the following:

1. He may declare the contract at an end and return the deposit.
2. Declare the contract forfeit and keep the buyer's deposit; however, this may create problems as to whether or not there is a cloud on the title.
3. He may sue for damages under conditions mentioned previously for the buyer.
4. He may ask that the buyer be required to perform or, in some areas, he may offer the deed and sue for the purchase price.

Although all contracts involve the basic elements already reviewed, the many special purposes for which contracts are prepared require special forms of, or additions to, the contents of the basic contract form.

If you and the buyer agree, you are ready to complete the transaction by signing a contract of sale. On some occasions the listing agreement can be signed as a contract of sale. Whatever you use, these are the basic elements of any:

CONTRACT OF SALE

If the buyer's offer is accepted the parties will then wish to complete a formal contract of sale which completes additional details not set forth in the deposit receipt—as, for example:

1. Disposition of personal property such as mechanical equipment, draperies, venetian blinds and similar items.
2. Exact method by which purchase price is to be paid. For example, a given amount received as a deposit, additional cash, and mortgage to be assumed, token subject to or to be secured.
3. Type of deed to be furnished, plus provision for proof of title and delivery of deed. The seller may have to be given time to clear the title and submit evidence that clearance has been completed for a given period of time.
4. Proration of taxes, assessments and insurance.
5. Date by which occupancy is to take place.
6. Proration of costs incident to the transaction, such as the drawing of legal instruments, recording instruments and services of those who aid in completing the legal technicalities.

(See Table 10-2 for suggestions about preparing to use a contract of sale.)

Financial Agreements

The heart of the contract of sale are the various financial matters which must be settled to the satisfaction of both parties. It is in this part of the negotiation that problems can arise which may negate the whole sale. Although they have been mentioned already, a review and comment will indicate why they are important:

Deposit. The deposit made by the buyer is usually a nominal amount, varying between five and ten per cent of the purchase price. If the buyer fails to perform as he has agreed to perform and if the seller has suffered damages, the seller may keep the deposit. Some confusion arises about this because the deposit is usually received by the selling agent, and because the amount is often equal to the commission he would earn for selling the property, he may assume that the deposit is his. It is not his; it is the seller's, and its disposition is a matter of agreement if the agent feels he should be compensated for his services. If the sale is completed the deposit amount is credited to the buyer as a part of the down payment which he must make. The receipt of the deposit is acknowledged in the deposit receipt and its form, i.e., cash, money order, check, should be noted, in order that it may be returned in the same form as received.

Down payment. In the usual sale a portion of the sale price is received from the buyer in the form of cash or its equivalent. The amount is usually determined by the difference between the sales price and the mortgage used to finance the purchase.

Mortgages. Eighty per cent or more of all single-family homes purchased annually are done so with the use of a mortgage, which is a device by which real property is pledged as security for the repayment of borrowed money. A buyer may secure a new mortgage, assume the mortgage existing on the property, take the property subject to the terms of the existing mortgage, or give a mortgage to the seller. When he uses a new mortgage he secures the borrowed funds from the lender and gives them to the seller in payment. When he assumes a mortgage he secures permission from the holder of the mortgage to take over the obligations of the previous owner. When he takes subject to the mortgage he agrees to make the payments on the mortgage, but the original borrower, the seller of the property, remains primarily responsible for the repayment of the mortgage. When a mortgage is assumed or taken subject to, the new buyer should ask for qualified statements of the terms of the mortgage and the amounts which have been paid to date on the principal interest.

The mortgage which the buyer gives to the seller as part payment on the purchase is known as a purchase money mortgage. In effect, the seller becomes his own lender and receives part of his purchase price in installments as the mortgage is paid off.

Table 10-2   Facts to Ascertain Before Drawing Contract of Sale

1. Date of contract.
2. Name and address of seller.
3. Is seller a citizen, of legal age and competent?
4. Name of seller's spouse and whether he or she is of legal age.
5. Name and residence of purchaser.
6. Description of property.
7. The purchase price.
    a. Amount to be paid on signing contract.
    b. Amount to be paid on delivery of deed.
    c. Existing mortgage, if any, and details thereof.
    d. Purchase money mortgage, if any, and details thereof.
8. What kind of deed is to be delivered: full covenant, quitclaim, or bargain and sale?
9. What agreement has been made with reference to any specific personal property, that is, gas range, heaters, machinery, partitions, fixtures, coal, wood, window shades, screens, carpets, rugs, and hangings?
10. Is purchaser to assume the mortgage or take the property subject to it?
11. Are any exceptions or reservations to be inserted?
12. Are any special clauses to be inserted?
13. Stipulations and agreements with reference to tenants and rights of persons in possession, including compliance with any governmental regulations in force.
14. Stipulations and agreements, if any, to be inserted with reference to the state of facts a survey would show: party walls, encroachments, easements, and so forth.
15. What items are to be adjusted on the closing of title?
16. Name and address of the broker who brought about the sale, the amount of broker's commission and who is to pay it, and whether or not a clause covering the foregoing facts is to be inserted in the contract.
17. Are any alterations or changes being made, or have they been made, in street lines, name, or grade?
18. Are condemnations or assessment proceedings contemplated or pending, or has an award been made?
19. Who is to draw the purchase money mortgage and who is to pay the expense thereof?
20. Are there any covenants, conditions or restrictions, affecting the title?

Table 10-2 *(cont.)*

21. What stipulation or agreement is to be made with reference to the Building Department and notices of building code violations?
22. The place and date on which the title is to be closed.
23. Is time to be of the essence in the contract?
24. Are any alterations to be made in the premises between the date of the contract and the date of closing?
25. Amount of fire and hazard insurance, payment of premium, rights and obligations of parties in case of fire or damage to premises from other causes during the contract period.

Escrow Agreements

In some states the buyer and seller may ask an escrow agent to assist in closing the transaction. An escrow agent is an independent third party who is furnished a copy of the contract of sale and given instructions to see that the terms are fulfilled by both buyer and seller. On the basis of the contract he prepares an escrow agreement which summarizes the duties of the parties and allocates all costs and financial obligations. The escrow agent may do nothing more than deliver the necessary papers to the buyer when the buyer meets all financial requirements; or the escrow agent may be asked to clear the title, probate all expenses including taxes and insurance, record the necessary legal instruments pertaining to the sale and do other tasks as instructed. The escrow agent can do no more than he is told to do in the escrow instructions, although some sales persons ask for his assistance in matters relating to the close of the sale.

Closing Statements

When an escrow statement is not used, a closing statement may be prepared as a convenient means of summarizing the duties of the parties. This statement is also derived from the sales contract and sets forth in detail, with exact dollar amounts, the obligations of buyer and seller. For example, such a statement might be as follows:

	Credit to Seller	Credit to Buyer
Total sales price	$15,000.00	
Deposit paid		$ 500.00

	Credit to Seller	Credit to Buyer
Taxes prepaid by seller	75.00	
Insurance prepaid by seller	125.00	
Mortgage assumed by buyer		12,000.00
Title clearance costs		35.00
Closing costs, legal fees	50.00	
	$15,250.00	$12,535.00
Subtract buyer credits	12,535.00	
Cash due from buyer	$ 2,715.00	

The decision as to who pays for such items as title clearance and closing costs varies throughout the country and is a matter of custom or negotiation, but the seller is always given credit for any amounts he has prepaid on taxes and insurance or similar items when they accrue to the advantage of the buyer.

PROOF OF OWNERSHIP

In order to provide the buyer proof of his ownership and to inform him about any restrictions (because of private agreements) you provide him with a deed of title which may be a:

Grant Deed

The grant deed receives the greatest use in the state of California. The deed must contain the word "grant" in mentioning the conveyance of rights. The deed has only four warranties or covenants: (1) the grantor or seller has not already conveyed the property to another; (2) the estate conveyed is free of encumbrances except as indicated; (3) no rights of way across the property nor building restrictions exist except as provided in the deed; and (4) the seller conveys any rights conveyed after the title passes. These warranties need not be expressed in the deed but they are always implied.

Warranty Deed

This is usually considered a better claim of title than the grant deed because of the "warrants" or "guarantees" that the seller of the property makes concerning the title. These warrants include: (1) a good and merchantable title; (2) the interests or use rights being conveyed; and (3) covenants or agreements to protect the buyer if he does not receive all of the rights which were specified in the title.

Quitclaim Deed

The quitclaim deed is used whenever the warranties of the warranty or grant deed cannot be certified. The quitclaim deed passes only the interest presently held by the present owner and warrants nothing with respect to the quantity or quality of the estate conveyed.

CONTENTS OF ALL DEEDS

The requirements as to the content and form of a deed vary from state to state, but these minimum qualifications are almost universal:

1. There must be a grantor, usually the seller and/or grantee, or buyer, and consideration.
2. The property must be adequately described.
3. The instrument must be physically delivered by the grantor or his agent.
4. The instrument must contain words indicating that the property is being conveyed or transferred.
5. The instrument must be signed by the grantor.
6. The instrument should also be acknowledged, although this is not required unless the deed is to be recorded. Acknowledgment is the formal declaration by a designated public official or a notary public that the deed is the act of the person or persons who signed the instrument.

In some instances the statute of frauds provides that an instrument that transfers title and mentions the amount of consideration is a valid deed, although it may not be classed as a warranty, grant or quitclaim deed.

Deed Restrictions

Deeds often include statements restricting the use of the property or the construction of improvements on the property. These are private contractual agreements covering a variety of items, of which the most typical are limits on minimum size or price of the house to be built, location of the house on the lot, limits on the number of families in the house, landscaping to be installed and many other kinds of restrictions. These restrictions may be enforced in courts of law by persons having residual interests in the property, or by an owner whose property interests may be affected adversely by a violation of these restrictions. Restrictions not in the public interest will not be enforced, and the Supreme Court of the United States has ruled that courts may not enforce restrictions denying ownership to persons because of their race or color.

Public Records

Public recording of instruments relating to property rights is used to notify third parties of the existence of rights in property and to establish the priority of rights or claims to property. Public recording is not always required, but is the conclusive proof in case of dispute over property rights. Recording consists merely of depositing the instrument to be recorded with a public official. The entire instrument is copied or photostated, together with a notation as to the time and date of recording. Usually the county recorder is responsible for all recording; however, the instrument must be recorded in the county in which the property is located.

The time and date noted in the instrument establishes the priority of rights, except that, if the person recording the instrument has personal knowledge of the existence of a prior claim not recorded, the act of recording does not give a priority of claim. In most states instruments most often recorded are ownership deeds, mortgages, mechanics' liens, and judgment liens. The authenticity of the signatures on the instruments to be recorded must usually be established or acknowledged by the proper state official.

USING LEGAL INSTRUMENTS
TO ACHIEVE INVESTMENT GOALS

Knowing how to thread your way through the legal jungle is a skill acquired only through careful study or from many years of experience. So, I repeat, do not try to be your own lawyer but do try to understand the many kinds of legal instruments you can use to achieve your investment objectives.

One of the first instruments you should know about is the *option*. Suppose you have found a property you may want to buy, but you want to check other details before you sign the sales agreement. To assure your right to buy on agreed-upon terms you can use:

Options

An option is merely a special form of contract in which the buyer makes a payment to the seller, in return for which the seller gives the buyer a stated period of time in which to decide whether or not to buy. If the buyer decides not to exercise his right to buy the seller keeps the payment. If the buyer decides to buy his payment may or may not be applied to the purchase price, depending upon the terms of the agreement.

What if you own a property but want to acquire another but for tax or other reasons you do not want to sell and then buy? What you must do at this point is arrange for:

Exchanges

Sometimes properties are exchanged in place of other considerations. This transaction gives rise only to changes in the wording of a standard contract to reflect the consideration involved. The key consideration in these contracts is the amount of cash involved, since obviously the two parties can set any amounts in their properties without injuring their positions. For example, if no cash is involved the property values can be equal and set at $100, $10,000 or $1,000,000, and neither party will have an additional amount to pay.

Perhaps you have found a property you would like to buy but do not have enough of a down payment, or you cannot secure a loan at present—what then? You might consider a:

Land Contract

Land contracts arise when the buyer for some reason does not have, or does not wish to pay, the full amount required for the down payment. It is usually provided, however, that after making a series of payments on the price they can then have the transaction changed to a normal sales contract. In this case the original contract will have to reflect this special condition. If the buyer is unable to perform he is usually released from further responsibility with his payments treated as rent.

If the buyer continues to pay on the contract but eventually wants to secure title and regular mortgage financing, the contract will typically provide that a given part of the monthly or periodic payment on the contract is applied against the purchase price. Even if no other financing is arranged, this permits the buyer to eventually acquire full title to the property.

The contract must be drawn to meet all of the terms of the agreement plus any special situations. The courts are particularly concerned about the rights of the borrower, and might well rule that a mortgage contract had been created. Important items include the type of title to be given, date and circumstances for receiving title and use, methods of payment, credits on equity and total price. Since the buyer is usually in possession of the property, he may be difficult to move in case of nonpayment, so that land contracts should be used with caution.

MORTGAGES AND TRUST DEEDS—FINANCING INSTRUMENTS

Whether you use a mortgage or a trust deed there are some elements common to both which you should understand before you agree to use the instrument. Some of the most important include:

The Property

Because the value of a property is related to the rights in it, the value of a mortgage is related to the quantity and quality of the property rights offered as security. For this reason, a complete and accurate description of all property is most important. For example, a property which includes a building owned by the borrower, plus lease rights to the land on which the building is located, when pledged as security has value only insofar as the lease rights permit maximum economic use of the building. For this reason, the property pledge should include a full description of the lease terms. There are also occasions when personal property may be classified as real property; however, whenever personal property is included on a mortgage pledge, the property should be fully described. A furnished apartment house, for instance, has more value when stoves, refrigerators, and washers are included in the real property description than when these are omitted. If such properties are removed, the rights of the purchasers may be subordinated to those of the mortgagor. Some mortgagees may even protect themselves by requiring that all personal property be secured by a chattel mortgage.

In some instances, property acquired after a mortgage has been executed will automatically become additional security for the loan unless specifically exempted by agreement.

The Debt

The mortgage debt determines the amount of lien interest which the mortgagee possesses in spite of what the note may recite. For this reason, the mortgage note must specify clearly the debt which is owed. This description usually means that a promissory note which sets forth loan terms (i.e., amount borrowed, method of repayment, length of loan, and interest rate) must be sufficiently explicit so that no other debt may be substituted in its place, and it must meet all the pertinent legal requirements relating to promissory notes (i.e., written form, parties with contractural capacities, pledge to repay a given sum on terms set forth, reference to mortgage clauses, legally given according to form, delivery and acceptance voluntarily).

The note is the key item in the mortgage transaction because, until it has been repaid, the mortgage exists and without it there can be no mortgage. The note represents a personal liability for the borrower and follows him until paid off. It is for this reason that a creditor can obtain judgments against other assets of the borrower if the sale of the mortgaged property fails to return enough to pay off the debt. The mortgagor and the mortgagee may agree that the real estate is the sole security for the debt, in which case deficiency judgments could not be secured. In other instances, since the note is a promise to repay a stipulated amount, personal judgments may be secured for any amounts not recovered through foreclosure.

The Pledge

The property is pledged as security for the debt, with the mortgage instrument which not only refers to the note and the debt, but also sets forth conditions under which the property is to be used during the life of the mortgage. Clauses dealing with this subject are often quite numerous and tend to vary according to local custom. The intent of these clauses is to guarantee that the property will always be maintained in a condition which will insure that there is sufficient value always present in the property to equal the amount of the debt not yet repaid. For this reason, the clauses require payment of taxes, or the mortgagee may do this and add these to the amounts owed; the property owner must carry property insurance with the mortgagee named as beneficiary; the property must not be altered, allowed to deteriorate, or otherwise abused to the injury of the mortgagee's interests; the mortgagee is given permission to enter the premises for inspection purposes. Although these clauses are printed in fine type and are often quite lengthy, they should be studied in order that the borrower may fully appreciate his responsibilities and rights.

The pledge is basically a specialized form of a business contract, with all of the requirements for legality of a contract, plus statements about the interest in the property which are mortgageable, the purpose of the contract, the pledging of the property, and the various clauses previously mentioned.

Priority of Debt

The priority of lien as between several mortgages held by private parties is determined by the date of the recording of the mortgage, regardless of when the proceeds are actually paid. Construction loans, for example, are paid out as work progresses, so that mechanics' liens might arise between payments. If the mortgage relating to the construction loan has been recorded prior to the recording of the mechanics' lien, it has priority even though the full amount of the mortgage has not been disbursed.

Additional Advances

Sometimes mortgages provide that additional amounts beyond those specified in the original note may be secured at a future time. If the mortgagee is required to make these advances, his lien rights are effective as of the date of the recording of the mortgage. If the mortgagee has a choice as to whether he makes additional advances, most states hold that his lien rights on these advances are subordinate to any other recorded liens; however, some states protect mortgagees even when optional advances are involved.

BORROWING TO PAY FOR YOUR INVESTMENT

Since the greatest profits in real estate investing are made by using borrowed money, many kinds of legal instruments have been used for this purpose. The major instruments are the mortgage and the trust deed (either or both are used throughout the United States).

Mortgages have been used to finance the purchase of real property for centuries and continue to find favor today, because of the numerous ways in which they can be adapted to fit a variety of lender–borrower needs. The modern mortgage has been refined by statute and interpretation so that it resembles early mortgages in only a general way. However, the mortgage is still basically a contract between the borrower and the lender which, within rather broad limits, can be written to suit their needs while protecting their rights.

The Mortgage

The mortgage is a device by which property is pledged as security for a debt. In order for a mortgage to exist there must be a debt, a property, and a pledge to repay the debt with the property offered as security for the fulfillment of the pledge. The person who borrows the money is known as the mortgagor, and the person who lends the money is known as the mortgagee.

The Trust Deed

Trust deeds are a special form of mortgage agreements but with some important differences. The unique feature of the trust deed is the use of three parties—the lender or creditor is the beneficiary, the borrower or owner of the property is the trustor, and the person who enforces the terms of the agreement is the trustee. The trustee has only sufficient title to carry out the terms of the contract once there is a default, whereas the trustor has possession and any rights to uses which will not injure the interests of the beneficiary.

Trust deeds normally do not carry either the right of redemption or deficiency judgments. When the trust deed is paid in full the trustor must ask for reconveyance of title. This reconveyance must then be recorded.

In other respects the trust deed resembles the mortgage. Actually, in some states the beneficiary may request that the trust deed be foreclosed as though it were a mortgage.

Custom in a community and state law will determine whether a mortgage or trust deed is used. In a period of declining prices the lender would gain from using a mortgage with its deficiency judgment provisions. On the other hand, in a period of rising prices a trust deed with its quick sale processes would be most advantageous.

Interest Rates

Rates of interest to be paid on the debt are stated in the note but do not necessarily have to be included in the mortgages. The majority of the states have laws which limit the rate which can be charged; rates above this are classified as usury and result in stiff penalties. Many states have broadened the usury definition to include loan costs, so that a rate could be usurious even if the state rate was not. This does not preclude a finder's fee paid to loan brokers who assist lenders in finding good loan prospects.

Fixed rate. Traditionally, the rate charged was fixed at the time the loan was negotiated and never changed, and most mortgages are negotiated in this manner.

Variable rate. In 1975 money prices were changing so frequently that some lenders began to use a variable rate mortgage. Under the terms of this mortgage the loan rate was fixed initially but could be changed up or down (usually 1/24 per cent every six months) according to changes in the costs of money to the lenders.

Fixed payment. In both of the above types of mortgages the monthly payment is a fixed dollar amount. However, in the case of the variable rate mortgage the amount is credited to reducing the amount of the loan. Of course, the length of time over which the loan would be paid would vary as the amounts allocated to the principal changed.

Acceleration

The mortgage contract and the note often provide that a default in payments automatically causes the entire remaining amount of the debt to become due. If this is not provided for, then separate actions of foreclosure have to be instituted for each monthly payment due. In practice, borrowers are often given 60 to 90 days in which to make up a defaulted payment. Foreclosure proceedings are costly and cumbersome, so that lenders are anzious to avoid them. For this reason, lenders will accept late payments; but this does not abrogate their right to exercise the use of the acceleration clause once they have named the debtor. Some debtors make a habit of prepaying on their mortgages. Whether these prepayments will apply on subsequently defaulted payments depends on the terms of the agreement.

Assignment of the Note

A mortgage note is a valuable property which can be bought and sold. Such actions do not affect the status of the borrower; however, unless he is notified to make payments to the new holder of the note, he may continue his payments to the original lender without jeopardizing his position. The process of selling the note is known as assignment.

Subordination

Subordination is the process by which the holder of a prior lien right agrees to give priority to a subsequent lien holder. The order of priority becomes important primarily in case of default, foreclosure, and sale of the property, at which time the holder of the earliest lien rights is paid first from the proceeds, and subsequent holders are paid until the proceeds are exhausted or all lien holders have been paid. Subordination agreements are created most often when a person buys a parcel of vacant land with the use of a purchase money mortgage. When the buyer seeks funds to build on the land, the holder of the mortgage on the land is then asked to subordinate his lien interests to those of the lender furnishing money for construction. There is a standard form available in most communities which can be used to accomplish the subordination, after which the agreement is recorded.

Recording

Although mortgages need not be recorded, in practice immediate recording is recommended following the signing of the mortgage agreement since recording establishes the priority of lien interests; except, of course, when a subsequent lien holder would have had personal notice of the prior liens. There are even some states in which priority in recording is the only basis for judging priority of lien interest.

Delivery

The legal requirements for the delivery of a mortgage are similar to those relating to deeds.

Satisfaction of the Mortgage

The obligations created under a mortgage may be satisfied in a number of ways of which the most common is payment according to the terms of the note.

Release

Payment of the mortgage note in full according to the terms discharges the mortgage; however, the borrower should ask for a return of the note and the mortgage agreement. In addition, a notice of release or satisfaction of the mortgage should be recorded in the place where the mortgage was recorded, in order to establish public notice of the release.

Since a mortgage is supported by a promissory note, the mortgage is worthless if the note is unvalidated. In some states, the note may not be enforced if no collection or effort to collect has been made for a period of time. When this happens, the mortgage has no value.

Foreclosure

When the note is not repaid according to agreement, the mortgagee may institute foreclosure proceedings which eventually result in the public sale of the property. Foreclosure starts with the mortgagee notifying the mortgagor that he is in default and action will be taken against him. After this, the action taken is determined by state law, but usually follows these steps: (1) a notice of action to foreclose is filed with the clerk of the county in which the property is situated; (2) any subsequent lien holders are given notice that they are defendants in the action; (3) the complaint which is filed sets forth the term of the note, the amounts due, and asks for a ruling that the property is to be offered for sale, and for right of deficiency judgment; (4) a copy of the complaint and a summons to appear in answer are then served on the mortgagor who is given time to reply; (5) if there is no reply a judgment is rendered on the amounts to be collected and a public sale is announced; (6) after the time prescribed by law, the sale is held, the costs of the foreclosure and sale are deducted from the proceeds, and the remainder paid to the mortgagee; (7) if the proceeds do not satisfy the note, the mortgagee then may exercise his right of deficiency judgment.

Foreclosure by Management

Sometimes mortgagees may prefer to avoid the expenses of foreclosure by including in the mortgage agreement provision for taking over the property, collecting rents, and managing the property until the amounts in arrears have been paid or the note has been satisfied. Mortgagees may also recover their interests by bidding at the foreclosure the amount owed to them, which means that they simply take title to the property.

Deficiency Judgment

Whenever the mortgage is not repaid according to schedule, sale proceedings may be instituted. If the sale fails to bring in sufficient proceeds to pay the amount still owed, the creditor may obtain a deficiency judgment against other assets of the debtor in an amount equal to that still owed.

Statutory Redemption

In some states, the mortgagor is given a period of time, up to one year, after the sale, in which he may recover his interest in the property by paying all amounts owed on the note, plus the interest due, plus all costs of the sale, plus interest on the total amount. In states where this is not permitted the period between notice of foreclosure and the sale may be delayed in order to give the borrower time to redeem his interests.

Military Persons

The U.S. Congress passed a law during the period of World War II that limited the rights of mortgagees to foreclose on persons who were in the armed forces. The title of the act setting forth details of this is the Soldiers' and Sailors' Relief Act.

Subsequent Lien Holders

Sometimes there may be more than one mortgage on a property, and the subsequent holders of these liens may feel that it is to their advantage to prevent the foreclosure and sale. In some cases, these debtors may take payments on the prior lien and add these payments to the amounts due them on their note. This will occur when a temporarily depressed market condition would produce a forced sale price too low to permit payment of all lien holders.

In Lieu of Foreclosure

Sometimes creditors and debtors wish to avoid foreclosure, so the debtor gives the creditor the deed to the property in lieu of foreclosure. This would occur only when the debtor's equity was nominal. Such conveyancing is usually evidenced by a document which indicates clearly that all of the interests of the debtor have been transferred to the creditor in return for proper consideration.

TYPES OF MORTGAGES

Since a mortgage is merely a device by which real property is pledged as security for a debt, the terms under which the pledge is made can be varied to meet a variety of financing needs. Some of the more common variations of the mortgage include:

Equitable.   There are sometimes occasions when property is pledged as security for a debt, but the instrument used in the process fails to meet all of the qualifications for a legal mortgage instrument. In most cases the instrument is treated as an equitable mortgage which is foreclosable in a court of equity. Courts have shown considerable interest in protecting the rights of borrowers, and will inquire carefully into an occasion in which some instrument such as a land contract is used to purchase land.

Deed absolute.   Sometimes a deed may be given in return for a loan, usually with the understanding that the deed will be reconveyed upon repayment of the debt. In cases where a dispute over the matter may arise between the mortgagor and mortgagee, the courts will examine the conditions surrounding the creation of the agreement to determine whether there was a sale and conveyance of deed or a loan transaction.

Purchase money.   Under the terms of this agreement the seller of the property takes back a mortgage as payment for the purchase of the property. Normally the holder of the purchase money mortgage does not have the right to a deficiency judgment.

Junior.   These contracts do not vary from an ordinary mortgage, except that the rights of the creditor are subordinate to a prior lien or mortgage.

Blanket.   Many times a large amount of money is borrowed and a single property is not sufficient security; therefore, several properties are pledged as security. As the mortgage is paid off the properties may be removed from the blanket.

Package.   The package mortgage is a recent development which has been coincident with the increase in air conditioners, automatic washers and similar equipment. Some lenders permit these and similar items to be included in the mortgage agreement as security for the debt.

Amortized.   Many of the foreclosures in the thirties occurred because the borrowers had the entire amount of the mortgage to repay at one time. In order to eliminate this problem home mortgage lenders now require borrowers to make periodic payments on the principal and interest, usually on a monthly basis.

Conventional mortgages.   These mortgages are not insured or guaranteed by a governmental agency.

Insured.   Mortgages whose repayment is insured by a third party. The most common type of insured mortgage is that used by the Federal Housing Administration, which insures lenders using their loans against a stipulated amount of loss if they lend on terms outlined by the FHA. The borrower is required to pay the premium on this insurance.

Guaranteed mortgages.   Mortgages whose repayment is guaranteed under much the same terms as those of the FHA mortgage, but the borrower pays no premium. The most common form is the Veterans Administration home loans (also known as GI loans).

Open-end.   Many borrowers must secure additional funds to repair, repaint, modernize or improve properties on which they have already placed loans. In order to avoid the incidence of subsequent mortgages, some lenders provide that the borrower may secure additional funds under the terms of the original mortgage agreement, with repayment extended to match the increased financial obligations. The priority of the additional debt depends upon whether the lender was obligated to make the advances, in which case the priority of the new debt coincides with the priority of the original agreement under which it was made, or whether the lender had a choice about making the additional advances. Priority of lien is often difficult to determine in some instances, so that many lenders avoid this type of mortgage.

Other Instruments

Although the mortgage is the most popular type of lending instrument, situations often arise when it is not the most useful type. Tight money markets, high interest rates or unusual types of investment situations may require other instruments.

Ground Leases.   On occasion a buyer may secure a long-term lease to land and erect his own improvements thereon. The buyer's rights are no better than those specified in the lease. For this reason, care must be used in selling lease terms and payments, providing for property improvement and use, and disposal of improvements owned by the lessee at the end of the lease. Such arrangements permit the lessee to avoid a heavy investment in land, and give the land owner a valuable improvement at the end of the lease.

Personal Notes.   Personal notes are merely unsecured promises to pay for the purchase of real estate. Usually they are for short-term use with a single repayment with accrued interest. They must meet the legal requirements for a note.

THE LEASE AS A FINANCING DEVICE

The tradition of property ownership is so strong in this country that many persons overlook the obvious advantages of leasing. The owner enjoys advantages because he may: (1) limit his personal investment in improving his property; (2) improve his property and guarantee a fixed return on his investment for a period of years; (3) secure some revenue from his property while he waits for property values to rise; (4) reduce or eliminate his costs of maintenance, repair, and modernization and his over-all property management activities. The tenant enjoys advantages because: (1) business tenants can secure the kind of property they need without tying up large amounts of their funds in land and buildings; (2) property use charges are for fixed amounts, which may protect the tenant in times of rising property use costs; (3) all leasing costs can be charged off as a business expense for tax purposes, whereas only mortgage interest and operating costs could be charged by owners; and (4) capital funds are free for selective investment instead of being tied up in fixed assets. There are other more subtle advantages which tend to attract a large number of sophisticated investors to this form of investment.

Purchase and Leaseback

The lease has become popular because it can be used in a process of purchase and leaseback which incorporates almost all of the advantages mentioned for both the tenant and the landlord. In the purchase leaseback process, an owner is given a long-term lease for a building he plans to erect on vacant land which he owns. He then uses the lease as collateral to secure long-term mortgage funds for constructing the improvements which the prospective tenant needs. A variation of the procedure is for the business firm to buy and improve a parcel of land and sell the property to an investor, while also signing a long-term lease for the use of the property. Thus the business firm secures the kind of building it wants and the investor has the lease, a collateral which he can use to finance his purchase. The success of this process depends upon the lease, the lessee and the tax position of the lessor.

The Lease

Leases cannot be used for mortgage financing unless they are relatively long-term in nature, which means usually that they must be written for periods of 30 to 50 to 99 years, or have an unexpired term well in excess of the term of the mortgage being used to finance the transaction. Care has to be exercised in drawing the lease, in cases in which the tenant is given the option of purchasing the property, since the courts may rule that the entire transaction was really a form of equitable mortgage arrangement. When repurchase is permitted very definite rules are laid down for determining the price and conditions under which the purchase may take place. This provision may also be tied in with one permitting a cancellation of the lease by the landlord. In all other respects the lease must conform to the requirements already mentioned.

The Lessee

Leaseback transactions are normally restricted in use to business corporations. Since the lease is to be used as security for a long-term loan, the tenant must be financially strong and have a reasonably long record of business success. Business concerns have been drawn increasingly to the lease for the financing of office buildings and commercial store properties, because the tenants in these structures often have special property needs, have excellent business performance records, but are notoriously loathe to invest their capital in real estate because they can earn so much more on it in their own types of businesses.

Tax Advantages to the Lessor

Tax advantages are present primarily in terms of federal as opposed to state income taxes, although the advantage to most investors is not very great. Leasing permits the lessor to recover his investment slowly over time, so that he does not have the large capital gains tax to pay that he would have if he had sold the property outright. The tax-exempt corporation which has no income tax to pay is most frequently attracted to leaseback contracts because it can lease back the property at lower rental rates (because they have no tax expenses) without sacrificing return on capital.

This advantage has been narrowed rapidly, however, and its early attraction which led many tax-exempt corporations into investing in this field has largely disappeared.

Problems of Leaseback Operations

The consummation of a successful sales and leaseback operation involves the extended use of a battery of experts; so the costs in time and money in completing such transactions are large. Furthermore, the advantages in such a transaction for federal tax purposes have been narrowed and reduced in increasing numbers, so that the appeal of more conventional financing methods is increasing. Perhaps the most obvious disadvantage of this process is the difficulty an owner may have if a large corporate tenant seeks modification of the lease, or is unable to make rental payments as scheduled. Not only would rental collection problems be compounded, but the problems of dispossessing the tenant would be enormous. Both lessors and lessees may ponder the advantages of this form of financing, as compared to the numerous protections provided them under the ordinary mortgage arrangement.

WHERE CAN I OBTAIN ADVICE ON MATTERS RELATING TO BUYING A HOUSE?

||||||||||||||||||||||||||||||||||||||||||||||||||||||||||||||||||||||||||||||||||||||||||||||||||||||||||||||||||||||||||||||

11

APPRAISERS

An appraiser is a person who, for a fee, will estimate the dollar value of a property. Home-mortgage lenders use appraisers to determine what the value of a home is in dollar terms since the amount which they can loan legally is defined as a percentage of the appraised value. Many appraisers are independent businesspeople who may be hired to make appraisal estimates by anyone who will pay their fees.

The appraisers' fees depend upon the amount of work which they are asked to do. The fee is never determined by the amount of value which they estimate for a property. Fees may range from as low as 25 to $50 for a minimum appraisal, such as the Federal Housing Administration requires for loan insurance purposes, to several hundred dollars for complex appraisals on the larger properties.

REAL ESTATE BROKERS (OR SALESPEOPLE OR SALES AGENTS, THEY ARE ALL THE SAME)

A real estate broker is a person who is paid a commission for doing specific work for a client, the work usually being that of selling a property. The fee is almost always expressed as a percentage of the price which is obtained for the property *sold*. Brokers are paid by the persons who hire them, usually the property sellers.

Buyers can also hire brokers although they do not often do this. Buyers who do not hire a broker to help have to visit many real estate offices and search out the type of property they wish to buy. In the bargaining process buyers should always remember that the broker will treat them fairly but the broker is obliged to seek the best possible price for the *seller*. Brokers usually specialize in selling only properties in the vicinity of their offices; therefore you should look for a broker with whom to do business who is located near the neighborhood in which you wish to buy a home.

Any person who sells property for a commission is licensed by the state. If the buyers or sellers feel that they have not been treated honestly they may report this to the state agency which licenses real estate brokers and the agency will investigate to determine whether the broker's license should be revoked. In some states, a broker's license is issued for those who are experienced and who wish to own and operate their own real estate offices and a salesman's license for those who have had only minimum experience and who will be working for a broker.

Selecting brokers is sometimes a very difficult process. Often your personal reactions to them are the best guide. However, you will also be able to get some advice by talking to the mortgage-loan office in the bank at which you do business. Many real estate brokers and salespeople belong to a local board of the National Association of Realtors. These persons are identified by the term "realtor." A realtor is examined for business qualifications before being allowed to join the board; and engages in a constant process of self-education and improvement and subscribes to a high standard of business ethics. A call to a local real estate board is therefore another means of finding a real estate broker with whom you can do business. The most effective real estate brokerage offices are usually those which have been located in a community for a number of years, whose members are part of a real estate board and other related professional groups and who are equipped to offer assistance in finding financing and other services you may need to complete the sale and have the property ready to occupy when you are ready.

LAWYERS

A lawyer can help you in preparing all of the legal papers connected with the sale of the property. A lawyer who is experienced in preparing legal papers can do a good job of protecting your interests, particularly when you are investing a large sum of money. In some instances a real estate broker may be able to help you on some points normally handled by a lawyer, as in the preparation of the sales agreement. A broker should never be asked to give legal advice; therefore, one of the indications of a good broker is knowing when you may need legal advice and will suggest that you should use a lawyer.

If you think that you may need legal advice, do not hesitate to call a lawyer, stating what you wish to know, if the answer can be supplied, and how much the charge will be.

CONTRACTORS

A contractor is the person who builds, repairs, and remodels homes. If you find a home that you think you may wish to purchase but which needs repairs or remodelling, you should contact at least one and preferably up to three contractors and ask them to submit estimates of what they would charge to do the work. You may also wish to ask them to give you the names of persons for whom they have done work so that you can see what quality of work they do. Before signing the contract for the work, you should also ask the contractor to give you one or two credit references whom you can call to determine if the contractor is financially responsible.

Home owners usually have two continuing problems with irresponsible contractors. First, the contractor may not be paying bills, and therefore lack the money to hire workers and pay for materials for your job; or may use in a careless manner the money paid for a job and not have enough to finish your work. Second, the contractor may agree to do more work for more persons in less time than possible so that your work may be started late or take an impossibly long time to finish. You can check on these aspects of a contractor's operations through the lending institution with whom you normally do business. You will also find that hiring a contractor who belongs to one of the several types of business professional organizations for builders and contractors is an effective way of finding a responsible contractor.

There are many types of contractors. General contractors will do almost any type of work related to construction. Other contractors specialize in plumbing, electrical work, heating, carpentry, masonry, painting, and in a variety of other activities. Be sure to select the right type of contractor for the work which you wish to have done.

ARCHITECTS

Architects will prepare plans for building a new home or repairing or remodeling an older home. Sometimes when the plan is rather simple you may find that you can use a draftsman rather than an architect. Architects are licensed and controlled by state agencies and professional organizations. The best architects are usually members of the American Institute of Architects (AIA) and should be used when you have a difficult problem preparing plans for your home.

Architects prepare plans, which are line diagrams of how your work is to be done, and specifications, which are lists of the materials to be used in the work and instructions on how they are to be used.

Architects' fees are usually established as a percentage of the cost of the work which they have planned. Sometimes they may be willing to do the work on a flat fee basis. Sometimes when you wish to be sure that the work is done properly you may want the architect to supervise the work. Architects also specialize and will do only certain types of work. You should let the architect know exactly what you want done and ask that the fee be quoted for you before work is begun.

Some architects draw plans and specifications only for buildings, others for parks, hospitals, and varieties of other kinds of construction. In addition to having a house architect you may also want to use a landscape architect who will advise on how to plan the use of your lot and the kinds of plants to use on it.

ENGINEERS

Engineers are specialists in construction and construction materials. You would use an engineer to help plan your house if you were planning to build on a hillside or other unusual type of lot. Engineers would help you if you wished to plan a house using steel or wood or other materials in unusual ways.

Just as is true of the other types of professional men, engineers specialize. You will find that there are electrical, structural, soil, foundation, and varieties of other types of engineers. You will find that you should deal with them in the same manner as recommended for working with architects.

TITLE COMPANIES

Title companies can tell you what kinds of use or other rights you own when you buy a home. They provide insurance for a modest premium which protects you against anyone else's claim on your property.

When title insurance companies do not exist, lawyers perform about the same kinds of services but give you an *abstract* and *opinion*.

ESCROW COMPANIES

In California a bonded (your protection against the company's errors, mistakes, failures) company supervises completion of all agreements and papers needed to transfer ownership. The company serves as a "stakeholder" to see that buyer and seller both do what they have agreed to do. There is a modest charge for these services.

When there is no escrow company (or even if there is one and you do not wish to use it), a lawyer provides the same services.

BUILDING—BUSINESS DEALINGS WITH THE ARCHITECT AND THE CONTRACTOR[1]

Some Principles of Trouble-free Building

1. Have a good set of working drawings and specifications that fit your site and needs. Have all work described adequately; be sure you know what is to be done, such as number of coats of paint, landscaping, and so on.

2. Let the architects accept bids from contractors they feel are qualified; don't force them to accept bids from any contractor. Never ask a contractor to bid just to get a bid; estimating takes time and money, often as high as $500 for one house.

3. Make written agreements with the architect and contractor, listing responsibilities and duties.

4. Deal with the architect and contractor, not with the workers on the job.

5. Call the attention of the contractor to all matters which appear to be wrong; get the matter settled at once.

6. Expect the contractor to finish work promptly and on schedule, but also recognize unavoidable delays.

[1]Based on Circular Series, Index Number A 20, 0, University of Illinois.

OBTAINING PLANS AND SPECIFICATIONS

From an Architect

A registered architect can be expected to furnish plans which are complete and accurate, the house well-planned and designed.

Plan Service Agency

1. See if the plans are from a competent architect or agency.
2. The agency helps you decide if the plans meet your needs.
3. Let the contractor or materials supplier decide on the adequacy of the plans and the specifications.
4. If you want changes in a stock plan, be sure an architectural draftsman is used; be sure contractor understands the changes.
5. The agency helps you look for builders who give "complete service" (plans, specifications, all building operations). Changes usually cannot be made in "standard" plans. The agency will not want you to make changes in standard plans because this usually means an entirely new set of plans will have to be drawn and the contract renegotiated. The agency will also check the "final" plans to be sure they meet all building code requirements and that costs include all plan items.

WHAT SHOULD BE INCLUDED IN SPECIFICATIONS?

The contractor is responsible only for what is in the specifications and drawings. Anything else added becomes "extra" over contract price. To be included:

1. Materials to be used and how to be used
2. All building operations classified under major headings:
   a. Excavating and grading;
   b. Concrete work;
   c. Masonry;

d. Carpentry and millwork;

e. Roofing and sheet metal;

f. Plumbing, heating;

g. Painting

3. Common practices sometimes misunderstood:

a. Electrical work includes installations, such as electrical outlets, and, if specified, connecting kitchen fan, furnace motor, electric range, and door bell.

b. Lighting fixtures may be purchased separately, the owner paying for them separately and paying for installation; or, a lump sum allowance can be provided with any savings or extra costs reverting to the owner.

c. Hardware specifications will include only rough hardware (garage and sliding door hardware, and all nails, bolts, and screws). Finish hardware will be covered by a cash allowance and selected by the owner.

THE ARCHITECT

Selecting an Architect

1. The title "architect" means the individual is competent as proven by examination, is registered and licensed. Designers and draftsmen usually have no license to practice architecture.

2. Talk to "satisfied" clients of architect.

3. Study types of houses done by various architects; select the one who designs and builds according to your tastes

Services Performed

1. Relates family's living needs to the building budget.

2. Draws preliminary sketches.

3. Prepares working drawings for cost estimation, if needed.

4. Prepares working drawings and details (exact dimension drawings showing floor plans, exteriors, structural details, mechanical installations). Blueprints are made from these drawings.

5. Prepares specifications.
6. Prepares contract forms relating to the work of the general contractor and sometimes for subcontractors.
7. Advise on selection of contractor—may assume responsibility for all construction—or may supervise.
8. Duties in supervision:
    a. See that work is carried out according to plans and specifications; assist in selection of hardware, lighting fixtures.
    b. Examine requests from owner, contractor, and subcontractor for changes and substitutions of materials; approves changes, issues orders for the changes.
    c. Check requests from contractor for payments and issues orders for payments in writing. Keeps accurate accounts.
    d. Final inspection of the job.
    e. Notice of completion, pay all bills, check for liens, issue orders for final payment.

Fees and Payments:

1. Design and supervision: 6–15 per cent of total final cost.
2. Design only: 3½–8 per cent.
3. Schedule of payments:
    a. On completion of preliminary sketches.
    b. On completion of working drawings and specifications.
    c. During construction (monthly).
    d. On completion.

Essential Elements of Owner–architect Agreement

1. Definition of relationship between owner and architect.
2. Description of architect's duties: time and method of paying fees.
3. Set forth owner's duties to include:
    a. Provide architect with information on restrictions, easements, boundaries, sewage facilities.
    b. Have survey made of site contours, grades, adjoining properties, streets.

c. Give prompt, careful consideration to all papers submitted by architect.

THE CONTRACTOR

Select a Contractor on Basis of (by Bidding or Reputation)

1. Financial resources, credit.
2. Reputation in general: integrity, cooperation, fair dealings.
3. Ability to complete job on schedule.
4. Experience and intelligence (past record).
5. Relations with labor, subcontractors, and material supplies.

Services Performed

1. Carries out provisions of contract document.
2. Orders and pays for materials.
3. Coordinates shipment of materials to site.
4. Awards subcontracts to various trades and schedules work of each.
5. Directs construction.

Fees and Payments

1. Lump sum payment: cost of entire house in this, any "extras" added.
2. Cost-plus, actual cost of materials and labor plus a fixed fee (usually 10–15 per cent of costs for overhead and profits).
3. Maximum total (rare): maximum total of house agreed on, including contractor's fees. Any savings are divided between owner and contractor.
4. Time of payment:
   a. Partial pay (when owner is financing or through an agency):
      (1) When foundation is laid.
      (2) When building is framed, roofed and enclosed—plumbing, wiring, heating installations roughed in.

(3) When plastering is completed.

(4) When building is accepted.

b. On completion.

Essential Elements of Contract

1. *Agreement:* all points agreed on by owner and contractor, scope of work, time and method of payment, and time of completion.
2. *General conditions:* duties and obligations of the contractor and owner to each other, duties of architect (if any) in relation to contractor.
3. Plans and specifications:
   a. All drawings needed for the work.
   b. Description of all materials and their quality.
   c. Description of work to be done and trades to be employed.

GENERAL CONDITIONS OF THE CONTRACT

These define the rights and responsibilities of the owner and contractor:

Contractor	*Owner*

Insurance and compensation
    Workmen's compensation;
    Public and private liability, property
        damage;
    Contractor responsible for any dam-
        age, injury due to his act or ne-
        glect or that of his employees.
	Fire and extended coverages during
	    construction should cover mate-
	    rials, scaffolding and stages,
	    cover materials, forms and mis-
	    cellaneous materials and supplies
	    for work but not tools.

Building Ordinances
    Must observe local, state, federal
        ordinances and laws relating to
        work;
    Must protect owner from all damage
        due to violation of these.
	Provided by owner.
	
	Property tax (usually only land dur-
	    ing construction.) Property tax
	    assessed after completion.
	In cost-plus, owner pays all taxes on
	    materials.

Permits
    City building permits: Either contractor or owner may take out—depends on local
        rulings.	

Utilities: Either contractor or owner may obtain and pay for—depends on utilities rulings.

Surveys

Taxes
Social security;
Taxes for materials, including sales
taxes;
All other state, federal, and city.

Other expenses of contractor
Labor, water, power, equipment, temporary heat, tools, and scaffolding during erection.
Sanitary facilities for workers.
Royalties and license fees; defends all claims for infringement of patent rights.
Pays expenses of protecting work from damage.
If requested: furnishes surety bond guaranteeing completion of contract and house.

Other responsibilities
Supervises the work continuously; requires correct execution.
Leaves house "broom clean."
Guarantees all work, makes good all defects due to labor or materials for one year or more after acceptance.
Responsible for all damage caused by negligence.

CONDOMINIUMS, COOPERATIVES, AND TOWN HOUSES

||||||||||||||||||||||||||||||||||||||||||||||||||||||||||||||||||||||||||||||||||||||||||||||||||||||||||||||||||||||||||||||||||||||||

12

A recent trend in home ownership has been the purchase of an apartment rather than a detached single-family home. This form of property ownership has many attractions and some pitfalls. Some special questions relating to this form of home ownership are presented as your guide to decide whether you might want to attempt this form of ownership that combines the qualities of single-family home and apartment living.

WHAT IS A CONDOMINIUM AND WHY SHOULD I BUY IT?

Condominiums, cooperatives, and town houses each have special meanings which we explain later; however, at this point I wish to discuss some common qualities which they have. For convenience I use the term condominium.

The condominium is a means by which several persons can join together to own and operate a residential living unit. The living unit can be built as an apartment house, several stories in height or as row housing. In any case land costs are reduced by placing more units on one acre of land than is possible with the typical single-family, detached house. For example, typical homes are built with 4 to 6 homes per acre but condominums can be built with twice that number, or even more per acre. For this reason most of the costs of a condominium relate to the dwelling space rather than land.

Most condominiums are built with open spaces, in which are placed swimming pools, golf course, picnic or recreation areas, tennis courts, and other improvements that enhance outdoor living. Frequently condominiums offer other services such as parking attendants, food catering, social activities, and maid service. The amounts and kinds of improvements and services offered depend upon what the owners in the condominium decide they want and will pay for.

In most units the tenants form a management committee which makes decisions about the operation and maintenance of public areas and facilities used by all of the tenants. The committee also sets budgets and determines how much each tenant should pay. Tenant management committees are usually the biggest source of trouble in condominium living. Preferably the management of the unit should be placed in the hands of a professional property firm. You should inquire very carefully into the way the condominium you wish is managed.

Most condominiums require that the purchaser of a living unit live in the condominium and will not allow leasing. You may also experience some difficulty in selling your unit since this form of ownership is not well known. On the other hand, more and more persons are being attracted to condominiums so that if you can avoid having to sell in a hurry you may find your purchase has been a good investment.

Simplified Definitions

Condominium: The ownership of an apartment, and sometimes land, through a recordable deed of title, plus joint ownership of common use areas and facilities. The owner is taxed on the apartment and partial interests in the common items.

Cooperative: The ownership of corporate stock that permits the owner to occupy an apartment and use common areas and facilities in the housing project. The owner of the co-op apartment must pay the corporation charges that cover taxes, mortgages, repairs, and maintenance.

Own-your-own: The ownership of a grant deed that gives the owner an undivided interest in the entire housing project and exclusive rights to occupy and use an individual apartment. (May be a condominium or a cooperative.)

Town house: The ownership by means of a recordable title deed of a lot and housing unit, which are part of a larger housing project consisting of a series of housing units joined with common walls; also includes joint ownership of common areas and facilities. Individual tax bills are paid on the apartments and proportional tax amounts paid on common areas and facilities.

WHAT DO YOU OWN?

(Only one of the sections applies depending upon form of ownership)

Good: 3 or more yesses; Acceptable: 2 yesses; Poor: less than 2 yesses

Cooperative

Do you own title to stock in a corporation that entitles you to the ownership of an apartment? If "yes," this is a cooperative apartment and you should obtain answers to the following:

	YES	NO

Do you receive an interest in land and the apartment, both of which a lender will accept as a security for your mortgage? Or do you receive interest only in an apartment?

Is provision made to require the corporation that owns the property to make payments on all encumbrances to the title of the property?

YES   NO

If one of the purchasers of an apartment fails to make payments, are the other purchasers liable for that share?

If other purchasers fail to meet their share of other obligations to be paid by all purchasers, are the remaining purchasers required to make the payments in their place?

Own-Your-Own

YES   NO

Do you receive deed of title giving you an exclusive right to occupy a particular apartment or unit and an undivided interest in all parts of the project not owned by a particular tenant? (This is a form of ''own-your-own'' ownership.)

What rights can you pledge as security for a mortgage loan? (Land, apartment, both?)

Do you face possible loss of your investment through failure of others in the project to meet their obligations to the project?

Can you obtain title insurance, or do you receive only a personal property right ''to occupy?''

Town House

YES   NO

Do you own title to a small lot and an apartment which are part of a series of small lots and joined apartments? (This is the town house concept.)

Does your right of title coincide with the boundaries of the lot and apartment that you purchase?

Do you receive rights to joint ownership of common landscaping, recreation, and other facilities in the project?

Do you incur other financial obligations relating to your joint ownership of ''common'' facilities?

(Note: You should ask for an itemized statement that represents a reasonably accurate estimate of your monthly/annual costs of ownership.)

Condominium

YES   NO

Do you receive title to a particular residential unit and a proportionate share or interest in the ''common'' areas? (This is condominium.)

Are all financial obligations, including property tax payments, segregated so that you cannot be held responsible for other obliga-

YES   NO

tions nor have your property title impaired because they fail to meet
their obligations?

Do your property rights exist "above the ground?" (They may and
this is normal in a condominium.)

Can you secure title insurance for your property rights? (If not this
may not be a condominium.)

RATING MANAGEMENT AND OPERATION

Good: 7 or more yesses; Acceptable: 5 to 6 yesses; Poor: less than 5
yesses

Has the corporation which owns the cooperative had experience in   YES   NO
owning and operating cooperatives?

Does the board of directors consist of a cross section of responsible,
experienced businesspeople such as lawyers, accountants, real estate brokers or developers, owners of businesses, and managers of
large businesses?

Does the charter provide, and have the directors shown (or appear
to have) the ability to: (Note: Court this question as a "yes" only
if you can answer "yes" to *all* these following.)

Elect capable, responsible officers.................................

Appoint effective operating committees ....

Supervise the management of the properties......................

Employ knowledgeable public accountants ....

Open, maintain and report on bank accounts ....

Adopt and enforce reasonable annual operating budgets ....

Fix minimal rental schedules for operating the co-op...........

Enforce house rules and the terms of the leases ....

Maintain the properties as pleasant living places ....

Improve the properties so that value is maintained..............

Establish and maintain fair rules for the sale or sublease
of each apartment or living unit.....................................

Do the stockholders, either by majority or two-thirds vote, have the right to decide or approve the proposed sale or sublease of each living unit?

Have the directors been effective in maintaining the annual operating budget so that the proprietary rent (the amount paid by the owner of each cooperative unit) annually is less than or competitive with the rent paid for similar units not under joint ownership?

Are the annual proprietary rents equal to or less than 10 per cent of the total purchase price of the unit?

Are the proprietary rents within the following ranges of percentages of the total rent charged?
(Note: Percentages should add to 100):

	Minimum	Maximum
Mortgage interest and amortization		15–30%
Real estate taxes		15–30%
Payroll for all employees		10–40%
Operating and other expenses		20–40%

Larger units pay more proportionately than smaller units for payroll and operating expenses.

Example: Cost of apartment unit $20,000
Annual range of costs $1,200–2,000
Owners' annual income $8,000

	Minimum	Maximum cost potentials
Mortgage charges	$ 300	$ 600
Real estate taxes	300	600
Payroll	120	800
Operating, other expenses	240	800
	$ 960	$2,800

YES   NO

Have the directors provided a financial contingency fund to take care of unexpected financial crises (disasters, inflation, or unusual repairs)?

Will the management company provide a year-end statement that reports the share of interest and real estate taxes that each apartment or unit owner can deduct for federal tax purposes?

Will the management company provide a year-end statement of contributions to mortgage principal payments so that you can determine your cost basis (original down payment plus principal payment) and your total present equity?

EVALUATING THE QUALITY OF LIVING

(Note: The use of "tenant" refers to the occupant-owner of the living unit)

Management of the properties   YES   NO

Good: 7 or more yesses; Acceptable: 5 to 6 yesses; Poor: less than 5 yesses

Is the management of the properties under the control of an experienced property management company?

Is supervision of the management company exercised through a tenant elected or appointed committee?

Is tenant approval required for the hiring of extra service personnel such as doormen, maid, and so on?

Is provision made for regular tenant meetings to discuss suggestions, complaints, personnel problems relating to the building staff, building maintenance, and standards of service?

Are regular inspections provided for to assure cleanliness of public spaces, condition of painted services, and efficiency of operating equipment?

Are detailed specification and more than one bid provided to the tenant committee for review and approval when extensive repair or improvement work is to be done?

Are vigorous and watchful efforts made to avoid violations of city laws or other regulations which might increase insurance costs of license and inspection fees?

Is every effort provided for to obtain the most advantageous terms of light, power, gas, fuel, telephones, and steam?

Will financing arrangements be sought when property improvements or repairs require extensive outlays?

Will efforts be made to represent tenants at hearings involving tax changes, utility rate changes, and assessed value of the property?

Are the charges for management services competitive to changes for such services in the local market?

Services provided

Good: 11 or more yesses; Acceptable: 8 to 10 yesses; Poor: less than 8 yesses

Is there a resident property manager who supervises the operation   YES   NO
and maintenance of common areas and facilities?

YES   NO

Are copies of all rules and regulations relating to uses of common areas distributed to all occupants; and are they enforced? (Yes to both is necessary.)

Can you register complaints about services and maintenance so that you can obtain immediate action?

Are you provided a list of services that are included in your basic annual rental or service payment?

Are you provided with a list of charges for special services and the nature of the services?

Are their penalties for your failure to maintain your unit according to the established standards; and do you accept them? (Yes to both is necessary)

Do the rules cover the following *(Who pays, how much, when the corrections are to be made and by whom?):
*Unless all rules are covered count the question as "NO."

   Broken windows, doors, and so on.

   Clogged or inoperative plumbing

   Electrical equipment

   Bicycle, boat motors, other equipment storage, and parking

   Extra keys

   Removal or changing of inner partitions

   Garbage, trash placement, and collection

   Pets and damage by pets

   Use of common equipment (replacement when damaged)

Is there a property management committee that meets regularly and to which you can address your suggestions or complaints about the operation and maintenance of the property and related services?

Special items to be checked in the unit you decide to select
   Good: 15 or more yesses; Acceptable: 12 to 14 yesses; Poor: less than 12 yesses

Are units soundproofed so that television, hi-fi, or party noises do   YES   NO
not carry through from the adjacent units?

Are you provided a view from your unit that does not include looking into adjacent units?

YES   NO

Is access to the doors of your unit protected by other limited access public doors?

Are you provided with extra bulk-storage facilities that will meet your needs?

Are walls between units fireproofed or fire resistant for at' least one-hour resistance?

Do you have reasonable privacy from the noises and view from public use areas such as swimming pools, game areas, and parking areas?

Can you be billed separately for all utilities, power, and so on that are exclusive to the use of your unit?

Are the following features provided (Yes or no to each):

Washer and dryer	Drapes
Air conditioning	Patios
Range	Fireplace
Oven	Intercom-music system
Garbage disposer	Swimming pool
Dishwasher	Play areas
Carpets	

Are tenants separated by age, family size, or children-in-family requirements?

Purchase and use conditions

Good: 14 or more yesses; Acceptable: 10 to 13 yesses; Poor: less than 10 yesses

Is there effective control over the partitioning or reduction in the   YES   NO
common use areas and facilities?

Are unit owners prohibited from removing their unit and their responsibilities from the common interests and areas?

Are individual unit owners who lose their units through fire, flood, or other means required to rebuild and to cover such potential through proper insurance?

Is the loss or damage of common areas and facilities covered through proper insurance?

Have ownership and use restrictions for the units and the property been properly recorded so that third parties are notified of these?

Can you sublet your unit and, if you can, are the conditions under which this may be done set forth clearly?

Can you sell your interest freely or have you been provided with clear statements of the conditions under which you may do so?

When you sell your interest can you recover your equity and any additional gains in value attributed to your unit and the entire property?

Are regulations clearly set forth regarding the painting, maintenance, alteration, and improvement of your unit?

Are regulations clearly set forth regarding the painting, maintenance, alteration, and improvement of public areas and facilities?

Are regulations clearly set forth regarding the landscaping and use of land around the unit which you own?

Are regulations clearly set forth regarding the landscaping and uses of land held in common ownership and use?

Have the directors stated what arrangements can be made if you fail to pay the monthly charges?

Will the directors or management provide assistance to you when you wish to sell your unit?

Will the tenants be given full advantage of all purchase, trade discounts, or other savings because of the ability of the property management company to buy in large quantities?

Is there space for entertaining large numbers for special events or parties that you wish to hold?

Will the property management assist you in obtaining catering services and other items you might need for entertaining large numbers?

Is there a committee or person charged with planning recreational and leisure activities for tenant groups?

Is the neighborhood attractive and likely to stay attractive?

FINANCIAL ANALYSIS

What is the total purchase price?

What is the down payment?

What are the loan terms?

> Number of years
>
> Interest rate
>
> Monthly payment

How much extra in percentage points have to be paid to get the loan?
(Note: One point equals 1 per cent of loan amount.)

What are the monthly common service fees (amounts paid by all tenants)?

What are the annual property taxes?

What are the annual property insurance premiums?

What other costs are associated with use and ownership of common facilities?

What are the monthly costs of extra car parking spaces?

SIMPLIFIED COMPARISON CHART TO AID YOU IN SELECTING "THE BEST BUY" IN COMMON OWNERSHIP UNITS

Form of Owner-ship	Total Units	Stories	No. of Bedrooms	No. of Baths	Square Footage	Price	Loan as Percentage of Price	Loan Payments	Service Payment

SELECTING A CONDOMINIUM PROPERTY MANAGEMENT FIRM

A major problem in owning a part of a condominium is that each owner has a vote in the management of the property, and most owners have little understanding of the property management process. Good property management should maximize your pleasure in using the condominium—your apartment and the public services, such as game rooms and swimming pools—and your opportunities to make a profit in the resale. A properly managed property can be as much an investment as any single-family home. Here are some suggestions:

1. The company selected should specialize in condominium management.
   a. It should be in business and have managed condominiums for at least five years.
   b. It should have an established office in a business building.
   c. It should retain experts in condominium management—either as a part of a larger property management organization or as a condominium specialist organization.

2. The company should be professional in its operations.
   a. It should be responsible for managing condominiums similar to yours.
   b. The condominiums they manage should appear to you to be operated as you wish to have your condominium managed. Visit them.
   c. Sufficient personnel should be available to meet both routine and emergency operations quickly, efficiently and inexpensively.
   d. An accounting system designed to meet the requirements of your directors and your particular type of property should be demonstrated.
   e. The company should provide errors and omissions, liability and other forms of insurance to protect the members of your condominium and your board of directors against loss in cases of legal and related suits.

3. Proper and complete management services should be offered.
   a. The company should maintain a general reputation among property managers for high quality management services. This can be evidenced by membership in professional property management organizations.
   b. The company should use mass purchasing power and labor teams which give you price and work advantages.
   c. A full list should be offered of all services it will provide and provision for changes in those services on a pre-established compensation basis.

d. A complaint-handling service that treats tenants humanely and competently should be provided.

e. A complete list of all services and fees for each, including the total fee, should be provided.

f. The company should identify all its subcontracts and the arrangements it makes to keep charges for all such services on a competitive basis.

RENTING YOUR COMDOMINIUM FOR INVESTMENT PURPOSES

Frequently the costs of purchasing a condominium are so reasonable that some will buy them for investment purposes. If you are thinking of doing this, here are some things to keep in mind:

1. Does the condominium agreement allow you to rent or sublet? If it does, what responsibilities do you retain and what responsibilities are shifted to your tenants?

2. Your rentals will be set by competition with apartment rental, so check your competition to determine your real rental potentials.

3. Check with the property management firm used by your condominium to determine if they will handle the entire problem of subletting, that is, leases, repairs and so on. You may be required to let the firm manage your rental.

4. Be sure that you consider all expenses: payments to the condominium for services, the utilities used by the tenants, and property taxes. Remember, all of these prices are rising, so anticipate such increases by providing that you and your tenants either share them or make certain that the responsibility for increases is well defined.

5. Do you want to think about a possible lease-purchase? If so, consider how the ultimate purchase price will be determined so that you can make a profit.

Note to Condominium Investing:

An investor saw a large condominium under construction in an area where the rental market was very good. When opportunities for purchase were announced, the investor placed $1,000 for each of ten units for purchase when finished. Eight months later the investor sold the rights to purchase for $10,000 each. A miscalculation would have resulted in either a loss of the original investment or the investor having to buy each of the units. Fortunately, the sales potential was correctly estimated.

LAND FEVER

||||||||||||||||||||||||||||||||||||||||||||||||||||||||||||||||||||||||||||||||||||||||||||||||||||||||||||||||||||||||

13

As you become more interested in real estate for investment purposes, you will begin to hear more and more tales about the fortune to be made with small investments in land. Perhaps you have heard or read about such opportunities: "Buy five acres in Lonesome Oak in the middle of an unspoiled wilderness. Visit the land with your family for a fun weekend and summer vacations. Put a small vacation home on it, and rent it out when you aren't using it. Let the rent pay for your investment. For only $1,295 per acre you will have swimming, riding trails, club house—all the fun of an expensive resort at prices you can afford."

Perhaps you can make a fortune in "raw land." Much more likely, with care, you can make it a pleasant second home or recreational experience for your family with very modest returns. Unfortunately, if you have any success with your first land purchase, you are likely to get "land fever," which means you may well be doomed to the eternal search for that one great "land killing."

Perhaps the most basic principle in seeking either good investment returns or a great fortune through land investment is to use only money you can afford to lose if the investment turns sour.

THE ATTRACTIVENESS OF LAND INVESTMENTS— CAPITAL GAINS

Those who recommend land as an attractive investment usually concentrate on only one aspect, the rapid, rich capital gains you can make. In effect, they are saying that if you can find raw land that is likely to be attractive for a number of kinds of improved uses in a rather short time (remember the "S" curve mentioned in Chapter 5?), you can make a large profit.

In a typical situation, a developer announces the availability of 5- to 10-acre plots in a remote area, usually either desert or mountain land, at ridiculously low prices, ($200–1,000 or more per acre.) The down payment is usually 10 per cent of the total price and the terms are a long-term loan, (perhaps 10 to 15 years), at a maximum rate of 10 to 12 per cent. Also promised are road and utilities to your property, perhaps a lake or river, horse riding trails, and a community club house. Sometimes these are provided, sometimes not. Too frequently they are provided slowly, and on a lot lesser scale than what you may have had in mind. Hopefully, you will make money because you buy early and then later take advantage of the interest of the large numbers of buyers who will come later. Unfortunately, many of these developments go bankrupt or simply never provide what was promised. Some have been prosecuted, fined, and the principals jailed. Some have survived because buyers make the down payments, a few monthly payments, and then quit paying when their profits are not realized. The company gets the land and sells it again, making its profits through these resales, the loan payment already made, and the high interest rates from the contracts which are fulfilled. Some of the developments do succeed as promised and the buyers do benefit, but they rarely achieve the very high profits they had anticipated.

How, then, are high profits made? Perhaps the simplest is to watch directions of growth, study the "S" curve and buy land on a wholesale basis with a minimum down payment. For example, suppose you buy 25 acres at $500 per acre, 10 per cent down ($1,250), and annual payments as low as possible. Within the first year you might try to sell one-half of your investment for the same price and terms as you agreed to for the entire purchase. In this way, your buyer is paying for your land.

HOLDING LAND WHILE WAITING FOR PROFITS

In calculating your profit potentials, you should consider the following:

1. Earning interest on your down payment.
2. Interest payments on the loan.
3. Costs of holding-property taxes and improvements (sometimes you may be required to add roads or utilities).
4. Costs of any improvements, utilities (water, electricity, natural gas, sewage disposal), and roads.
5. The profit you wish to make.
6. Costs of transferring the title when you buy and sell.

All of these costs must be subtracted from any difference between what you pay for the property and what you receive. Under typical circumstances, you might find that the annual costs equal these percentages of the market price:

	Annual Rates
1. Earning on your down payment (10% earnings × 10% down)	1%
2. Interest on the loan (10% × 90% loan)	9
3. Property taxes	3
4. Improvements (2% of total value)	2
5. Profits you wish to make on total investment	12
6. Costs of transfer (commission plus legal costs)	11
	38%

Thirty-eight per cent may seem unreasonably high, so substitute the actual figures for any raw-land investment you are contemplating and you will find that such investments must earn a very high rate of value increase each year if you wish to make the higher profits associated with such risky investments.

HOW MUCH IS THE LAND WORTH?

Estimating what you should pay for raw land is extremely difficult to do. You should do a lot of shopping around to find out what others are paying. Particularly, you should talk with sellers to see what they paid when they purchased and what they hope to make. Talk to buyers to determine whether they are experienced, knowledgeable buyers who have made good estimates of what they can earn or whether they are inexperienced buyers hoping to make a ''killing.'' To help you decide what to pay, examine Table 13-1.

Table 13-1 Methods of Estimating Land Value

Market comparison (vacant land only):
Use market comparison approach but
use *only vacant lots* comparable to that
being appraised. $ _____

Assessed value ratio:
Typical sales prices in area. $ _____

Typical assessed values. $ _____
Average sales price divided by average assessed values. $ _____

Assessed value of lot being appraised
× sales assessed value ratio. $ _____

Land residual:
1. Typical sales prices in area. $ _____
   Typical cost to construct a building
   similar to the one being appraised
   but without any depreciation. $ _____

$$\frac{\text{Land value}}{\text{Market}} =$$ Sales prices minus cost of all
improvements, including the building
and all sales and transfer costs. $ _____

Table 13-1 *(cont.)*

2. Estimated net income of property. $ _____

Minus: building
cost of new minus depreciation
× capitalization rate. $ _____
Net income earned by land. $ _____
Land value   = Land income divided by
‾‾‾‾‾‾‾‾‾‾‾‾‾‾‾‾
Income capitalized   interest rate

Market activities:

How many parcels are being sold currently and
with what price ranges?   _____

What experiences have previous purchasers of
similar land had in trying to resell?   _____

Is there any kind of development going on
on the land purchased earlier?   _____

How many purchasers have resold and what
experiences have they had?   _____

Will the seller furnish government reports that
tell about expectations with respect to the land?   _____

TYPES OF LAND INVESTMENTS

There are many types of land that can be purchased for investment. Remember that land has value because it can be used for
something—homes, industry, parks, or government. The kinds of
things for which land can be used relate to its location; therefore, return
to Chapter 6 on location and study it carefully and match it with
Chapter 5 on the "S" curve. In this chapter we will concentrate on a
few of the more evident kinds of raw-land investments. Presumably,
you buy this land for resale as land and you do not intend to engage in a
development process. You plan to buy land at wholesale prices and sell
it at retail.

Remote Land with Recreational Potentials

Suppose that you do find an irresistible chance to buy some very
attractive raw land that will be developed for recreational purposes. In

Table 13-2 is presented a typical format for analyzing such land for investment purposes, using hypothetical (but realistic) amounts, Without consideration of the development problems, notice the potentials for an equity increase for the raw land.

Table 13-2   Underdeveloped Land as an Investment

Assumptions:	
Price per acre	$1,000
Down payment	100
Loan	9,900
Terms: 15 years at 9 per cent	
Monthly payment	100.41
Annual payment	1,204.95
Brokerage commissions 15 per cent sales price	$150
Maintenance, additional cost of 1 per cent original value annually	$10

Holding costs	*Percentage of original price*
Mortgage payments (price and interest)	12.17
Property taxes	2.75
Return on equity 10 per cent (on down payment)	1.00
Maintenance, other holding cost	1.00
Annual holding costs as percentage of original price	16.92

Assume 20 per cent annual price increase

Assume a 5 year holding period and sale

	Total	*Annual average*
Price increase	$14,883.20	$2,976.64
Brokerage commission 10 per cent	2,488.32	497.66
Net after commission	$12,394.88	$2,478.98
Total tax (3 per cent annual increase)	1,460.02	292.00
	$10,934.86	$2,186.98
Mortgage interest paid	3,977.12	795.42
	6,957.74	$1,391.56
10 per cent on original equity	61.05	12.21
	$6,896.69	$1,379.35
Maintenance and holding costs	61.05	12.21
1 per cent on original price		
10 per cent earnings		
	$6,835.64	$1,367.14
Original equity	100.00	

Table 13-2 *(cont.)*

Price increase (equity increase)	14,883.20	
Equity buildup, mortgage	2,073.46	
	$17,956.66	

Assume 10 per cent annual price increase, 5 years holding period.

	Total	Annual Average
Price increase	$6,105.10	$1,221.02
Brokerage commission 10 per cent	1,610.05	302.01
	$4,495.05	$ 919.01
Mortgage interest paid	3,977.12	795.42
	517.93	$ 123.59
10 per cent on original equity	61.05	12.21
	$ 556.88	$ 111.38
Maintenance holding cost	61.05	61.05
	$ 495.83	$ 50.33
Original equity	$ 100.00	
Price increase	6,105.10	
Equity buildup, mortgage	1,973.46	
Equity increase	$8,178.56	

On the other hand, suppose that you want to participate in the development of the land to its full recreational potential. Table 13-3 is, again, a hypothetical but realistic dollar presentation of such a development. Notice that during its early years the development loses money. This is because of the heavy investments that must be made in the improvements necessary to prove to eventual investors that the project will develop. If you want an income tax loss, this is attractive. Otherwise, you may have to wait for some time to make "real" profits.

Table 13-3 Recreational Land Development Feasibility Study

Basic Data Inputs

Total land purchased	100 acres at $2,000 per acre = $200,000
Lot sizes (in acres)	.50
Per lot income/sales/cost potentials	
Price (annual increase of 15 per cent)	$ 5,000
Down payment	500
Land contract—10 per cent per year for 10 years	
(monthly payment $59.47: average annual total)	714

Table 13-3 *(cont.)*

Sales commission (15 per cent)	750
Advertising (annual for unsold inventory)	50
Closing costs received	100
Closing costs paid	80
Recreational facilities, services income	150

Development costs (per lot)
Initial

Down payment	20,000
Site preparation, grading, roads	100,000
Utilities to lots	100,000
Recreational lake and facilities	100,000
Clubhouse	50,000

Holding costs: development period of 5 years
Property taxes .02 per cent of market value: annual increase of 10 per cent

Land mortgage payments	Loan amount	$180,000
	Term	5 years
	Interest rate	10 per cent
	Annual payments	$47,484

Property maintenance, operations sites ($50 per site per year, unsold inventory)
Lake, clubhouse, recreational facilities (annual) $15,000
Project management 5 per cent of gross sales

Assumptions:
All facilities in and ready to use at end of first year
Lot sales in first year, 10 per cent discount, no membership fees collected

			End of Year		
	1	*2*	*3*	*4*	*5*
Earned Income (price per lot)	5,000	$ 5,750	$ 6,612	$ 7,604	$ 8,467
Lot sales	$ 90,000	$287,500	$396,720	$456,240	$ 84,670
Recreational memberships ($100 per year per lot)	0	7,000	13,000	19,000	20,000
Recreational related sales	0	10,500	19,500	28,500	30,000
Closing costs received[1]	2,000	5,000	6,000	6,000	1,000
Potential earned income	$ 92,000	$310,000	$435,220	$509,740	$135,670
Lot inventory					
Beginning	200	180	130	70	10
Sales	20	50	60	60	10
Start of next year	180	130	70	10	0
Cash Flow Analysis					
Lot down payments	$ 10,000	$ 25,000	$ 30,000	$ 30,000	$ 5,000
Mortgage payments[1]	14,280	49,980	92,820	135,660	142,800
Other cash income	2,000	15,500	25,500	34,500	31,000
Cash flow total	$ 26,280	$ 90,480	$148,320	$200,160	$178,800

Table 13-3 *(cont.)*

Counting all lot sales as of first of year although they will be sold at different times in the year.

Expenses					
Initial					
Down payment, raw land	$ 20,000				
Site preparation	100,000				
Utilities	100,000				
Recreational facilities	100,000				
Clubhouse	50,000				
	$370,000				
Holding Costs					
Property taxes	$ 4,000	$ 4,400	$ 4,840	$ 5,324	$ 5,856
Property maintenance					
Sites	9,000	6,500	3,500	500	0
Improvements	15,000	15,000	15,000	15,000	15,000
Sales commissions	15,000	43,125	59,508	68,436	12,700
Advertising	9,000	6,500	3,500	500	0
Closing costs paid	1,600	4,000	4,800	4,800	800
Project management	4,500	14,375	19,836	22,812	4,233
Loan payments	47,484	47,484	47,484	47,484	47,484
Holding costs total	$105,584	$141,384	$158,018	$164,856	$ 90,306
	370,000				
	$475,584				
Gain or (Loss)	($449,304)	($50,904)	($ 9,698)	$ 35,304	$ 45,364
(Cash flow minus holding costs)					

[1]All cash received treated as current income.

Urban Fringe Acreage

Urban fringe acreage is a very attractive form of land investment if you know how to judge directions of city growth. Again the ''S'' curve analysis will be useful. To this curve you must add a realistic time dimension. How fast are streets, water, power being added? How quickly is the land being developed? Who are the developers and how successful have they been?

Some basic ideas to help you include:

1. Buy near large traffic intersections.
2. Anticipate growth by watching where water and sewer lines and streets are being installed or are to be installed. Most cities usually give yearly capital improvement budgets which tell precisely what they intend to do.
3. If many homes have been added, look for a vacant parcel on which to place stores or shopping centers.

4. Near major streets, rail lines, highways, freeways look for vacant land in small parcels which might be assembled to make a large parcel.

5. In a developed residential area look for unusual or overlooked parcels. Find the owners and talk to them. They may not know what can be done, or they may need help in doing it. Offer to cooperate in a venture.

6. In older areas that are changing to other uses, observe the new uses. Try to assemble some of the poorer looking properties and plan for their reuse.

PRINCIPLES OF BUYING LAND

There are many principles to be followed found throughout this book. At this point remember these which apply particularly to land investments:

1. Keep your down payment and investment capital small.

2. Encourage the sellers of the land you are buying to participate in the process and share in the costs and risks.

3. Use options to acquire the right to buy land and use the option period to get the financing and participation of others.

4. Watch parket changes and plan the right time to buy and sell; do not see land as a long-term investment unless you are very rich.

5. Stuay local area changes carefully so that you can anticipate land use changes.

PITFALLS OF LAND DEVELOPMENT

You may be tempted to join with others to develop land that you feel is ripe for improvement. Again, there are some principles to keep in mind:

1. Increasing numbers of government regulations are being introduced to control land development at the city, county, state, and federal level. More and more require detailed reports on what is intended and how the development will affect various aspects of the environment. These can delay development by as much as 36 months.

2. Private agreements, in the form of deed restrictions, may prevent the development as you plan it.

3. The costs of development are increasing rapidly each month. Many developers or contractors will no longer accept firm price contracts for their work. Costs are extremely difficult to estimate.

MAKING MONEY BY LOSING MONEY: THE BASICS OF FEDERAL INCOME TAX LAW

||||||||||||||||||||||||||||||||||||||||||||||||||||||||||||||||||||||||||||||||||||||||||||||||||||||||||||||||||||||||||||

14

You are probably generally aware that federal income tax law can help real estate investors. Perhaps you are taking full advantage of such deductions as mortgage interest and property taxes. The law is complicated and changes annually so that at best you can gain an appreciation of how to use the law, but for serious investment purposes you will want to use a knowledgeable tax expert.

BASIC PHILOSOPHY

All income can be taxed by the federal government, although congress has provided for many types of exemptions. Income can be taxed when it is earned by the sale of goods and services, and when it is

162

earned because of an increase in the value of an asset when the increase is received as cash (capital gains).

Income earned from sales of goods and services is taxed at the highest rates, but many deductions can be taken before the amount to be taxed is calculated. Income earned from the sale of an asset is taxed at a lower rate, but fewer deductions can be taken from the profit realized. However, you cannot take advantage of the capital gains provisions unless you have owned the asset for at least six months.

Since there are several things you can do to influence the amount of income to be counted as either earned or capital gains income, real estate investors have these basic rules:

1. When you expect a gain (either earned or capital value), try to get a maximum amount of the income counted as capital gains.
2. When you expect a loss (either earned or capital value), try to get a maximum amount of income counted as earned income.

Our concern in this chapter is with the tax advantages associated with buying and selling homes, and we shall concentrate on that, even though the other aspects related to income-producing properties are fascinating, and a source of added wealth.

THE HOME OWNER AND FEDERAL INCOME TAXES

Whatever your earned income, there are some important deductions allowed to home owners which you should always use:

1. All interest paid on mortgage loans can be deducted from the earned income before you calculate the income taxes you owe.
2. All property taxes paid can be deducted.
3. Uninsured losses to your home can be deducted. This portion of the law is complicated, but keep track of all losses—from fires or floods, as well as losses due to possible neglect or error.

When you sell your home, you must account for differences between the price you paid for the home, any capital improvements which you have made, and the price you receive from the home. For example:

Original purchase price $20,700

Improvements you have made 3,500
    Landscaping and walks = $1,000
    Change in heating system,
       including air condition = $2,500

Costs incidental to sale
    Commissions and improvements 2,800

    Tax basis $27,000

Sales price..$35,000
    Difference subject to capital gains tax $ 8,000

The amount of tax that you will pay depends upon your tax bracket, but in no case can it exceed the capital gains rate, which is now about 25 per cent. If this had been earned income, you might have paid as much as 35 per cent or more.

Income from real estate investments is added to other earned income to determine what tax rate and amount you pay. For example if your total taxable income from other than real estate requires you to pay 35 per cent on your tax reportable earned income then that rate is applied to any income earned from real estate. However, capital gains are not considered to be earned income and are taxes at a different, usually lower, rate.

However, there is more good news. If you sell your home but buy a new home within 12 months or build a new home within 18 months of the time you made the sale, and the price is equal to or greater than your sales price, there are no federal income taxes due.

If you have built up an equity in the home and trade for an equivalent equity, you also have no tax to pay. For example, suppose that you have an equity of $20,000 in the $40,000 home you sold and you trade for a $60,000 home using your equity as a down payment, you have no tax equity at that time. You have no taxes to pay until you receive cash or its equivalent.

You can also postpone some of your liability by accepting a down payment of less than 30 per cent of the sale and the remaining payments are made in two or more payments. Your gain is figured in proportion to what you receive, and you pay the taxes only in the year in which you receive the payments. For example:

Sales price = $40,000
Down payment received = $8,000
Annual payments = $8,000 for 4 years
Total gain = $8,000

Gain to be received and reported annually = 20 per cent of $8,000, or $1,600.

Remember, you must have owned the property for at least nine months, or all this income must be reported as earned.

If you happen to own more than one property and sell one for a gain and one for a loss, you can deduct the loss from the gain under given conditions. The process is complicated and I suggest that you merely keep in mind that it *can* be done, but an expert should be consulted in determining your taxes.

Perhaps you are thinking of using your real estate to produce added earned income. In this case, you may choose to convert your home to a rental unit and use it for investment purposes. This enterprise is really beyond the scope of this volume, but briefly, here are the advantages and problems:

1. All expenses incidental to renting can be deducted from the rents received.
2. An amount representing depreciation of the building can be deducted from income, even though there may be no income loss from depreciation.
3. The rents charged must be competitive.
4. You can then exchange the home for another rental unit of a larger size and not necessarily for another home.

Some Precautions

You can use your home for income tax protection only under certain circumstances which you should remember:

1. If you regularly buy and sell real estate and receive earned income regularly from such sales, you may be considered to be in the real estate business and all income from such sales will be treated as earned income.

2. If you use real estate as a part of a business or trade, it becomes subject to federal income taxes affecting businesses.

3. You must be able to establish both through records and the treatment of your property that you are holding it for investment purposes or for the production of income.

PRINCIPLES OF USING INCOME TAX LAWS EFFECTIVELY

Perhaps the most important principle is that you will need an expert to help you estimate your income tax liabilities. Such experts are normally lawyers or accountants. Before you begin to work with this expert, discuss your problems at some length to be sure the expert has the knowledge and experience to understand and help you solve your real estate problems. Determine that the expert is professionally competent by degrees (law) or by earned certificates held (CPA), and by clients serviced (ask to talk to one or two).

Income tax laws change, as well as the interpretations of their meanings annually, so use your experts every year to prepare your tax returns. However, bring the expert in at the beginning of the transaction so that you can obtain all possible advantages and tax shelters.

Since the home is a part of your family estate, you may want to consider other factors that will affect your decisions about using a federal law. For example, there are state laws, license laws, franchise taxes, sales taxes, and trust arrangements that should also be considered when you are planning your income tax strategies.

In any given situation, several portions of the federal tax law may affect your property. An expert will help you find all such regulations and recommend how you work with them.

Remember, your goal is to leave yourself maximum opportunities for choosing how and when you pay your taxes. Never are you to try to evade payment; this is illegal.

RECORDS

Keep full, complete, accurate records of all transactions affecting your home's value or price: copies of contracts, escrow papers and bills paid. When you pay a bill relating to your home, insist on a receipt that identifies the firm, its location, and all materials and services paid for. A cancelled check is rarely sufficient evidence of a bill, but do keep all cancelled checks and attach them to the bills to which they relate.

Do not assume that an expense related to your home cannot be used in some financially advantageous manner. Keep all your bills and show them to your expert at the end of the year and let the expert tell you what to keep. Equally important, discuss large expenditures ahead of time with the expert so that you can use them to your advantage. For example, capital improvements can be added to the tax basis to reduce your tax liability. If you are thinking of reroofing, making plumbing changes, or similar expensive undertakings, find out how to take advantage of federal tax law to get tax credits.

Perhaps the most fortuitous aspect of federal income tax law is that it places no penalties on you if you lose money as an investor. If you pay interest which is above the market rate, incur unusually heavy improvement expenses, and so on, you can still use the tax laws to your advantage.

There is one final example in terms of investment planning. Suppose you are earning an income that places you in a high income bracket. You might buy a home that is in need of repairs for rental purposes. Each year you plan improvements and other expenses for the rental of the property, so that you lose money on the rental. In fact, each year you have to deduct these losses against other income. If you have purchased the property and improved it so that its capital value increases regularly, and at the time you may need some cash you can sell the improved property and have only a capital gains tax to pay. In other words, by losing money you have made money.

BRINGING IT ALL TOGETHER— INVESTMENT PRINCIPLES

||||||||||||||||||||||||||||||||||||||||||||||||||||||||||||||||||||||||||||||||||||||||||||||||||||||||||||||||||

15

Suppose you are convinced that your home should be used for investment purposes but still feel somewhat shaky about your abilities to do this. Perhaps these summary ideas or principles will help you sort out what to do, when to do it and how to do it:

1. Successful investing requires the use of borrowed funds. Do not hesitate to use other people's money and to keep your equity low when inflation is pushing up prices and you can borrow money at a fixed rate.

2. Be sure to use the advice of experts in planning and managing your home as an investment. The experts and their responsibilities include:

    a. Appraisers: to recommend the investment value;

    b. Contractors: to identify and estimate for you the costs of improving, modernizing, repairing;

   c. Mortgage lenders: to advise you when, where, and how much to borrow, and on what terms and at what rates;

   d. Real estate brokers: to help you identify good investment buys and the right prices and terms on which to buy (as well as rents to charge if you decide to try rental-investment approaches); and

   e. Tax counselors: to work with you in planning all possible income tax advantages.

3. Buy only homes you have personally inspected, located in areas that you have visited and studied thoroughly.

4. Keep informed on changes occuring in property uses and in prices. Plan to change your ownerships to fit market changes.

5. Maintain the capital value of your home through a sensible program of maintenance and repairs.

6. There are many ways of financing your purchase, and many differences in what financing will cost, so do not hesitate to shop for money.

7. Financing can be secured from many sources, so do not inquire only at banks and savings and loan associations. Be sure you also compare all of the costs and terms.

8. Each investment is unique and may not behave according to "typical" market changes.

9. You must expect to pay continuous personal attention to your investment and, in the process, may learn about house repairs, maintenance, loans, all of which are associated with treating your property as an investment.

10. Do not "fall in love" with a particular property. Remain objective, keeping in mind that investment objectives may require you to buy less than what you might "like" and to sell even though you like the property very much.

11. Keep your investment objectives in mind and make sure you are managing your home in terms of these.

INDEX

A

abstract and opinion, 95
acceleration, 115–16
access, 65, 72
    to bathroom, 73
acknowledgement, 107
actual price paid, 35
address, 34
advances, additional, 113
advantages, of home ownership, 115, 166
affording home, 17–27
age, 32, 35
    of fixtures, 75, 76, 77
    of home, 15
agreement, 134–35
air conditioning, 77
alterations, 24, 104
American Institute of Architects, 129
amortization, 121
appearance, 66
appliances, 26
appraisal:
    fees, 23
    report, 33
    yours, 34 (checklist)
appraisers, 2, 29, 126
approach, 77
architects, 129–30, 132
    fees and payments, 134
    selection of, 133
    services of, 133–34

Architectural Forum, 89
architecture, 64
area, 15, 71, 72
arrangement of rooms, 64
artificial light, 74
assessed value, 66
assessments, 24, 104
assignment of note, 116
assumptions, 103, 104
attorneys, 99
auto, 75

B

back yard, 76
banks, 12, 45
bargain and sale, 104
basement, 68
bathrooms, 68, 73–74 (checklist)
bedrooms, 67, 72–73 (checklist)
    with baths, 15
block books, 92
Board of Governors, Federal
      Reserve System, 86
booms, topping out of, 51
boundaries, 56
breezes, 70
broker, 104
    commission, 23, 97
    hired by buyers, 127
    other offices, 34
builder's capabilities, 82